T0318710

Cambridge Elements ≡

Elements in Perception
edited by
James T. Enns
The University of British Columbia

THE BREADTH OF VISUAL ATTENTION

Stephanie C. Goodhew
The Australian National University

CAMBRIDGE
UNIVERSITY PRESS

CAMBRIDGE
UNIVERSITY PRESS

University Printing House, Cambridge CB2 8BS, United Kingdom

One Liberty Plaza, 20th Floor, New York, NY 10006, USA

477 Williamstown Road, Port Melbourne, VIC 3207, Australia

314–321, 3rd Floor, Plot 3, Splendor Forum, Jasola District Centre,
New Delhi – 110025, India

79 Anson Road, #06–04/06, Singapore 079906

Cambridge University Press is part of the University of Cambridge.

It furthers the University's mission by disseminating knowledge in the pursuit of
education, learning, and research at the highest international levels of excellence.

www.cambridge.org
Information on this title: www.cambridge.org/9781108796217
DOI: 10.1017/9781108854702

First published 2020

A catalogue record for this publication is available from the British Library.

ISBN 978-1-108-79621-7 Paperback
ISSN 2515-0502 (online)
ISSN 2515-0499 (print)

The Breadth of Visual Attention

Elements in Perception

DOI: 10.1017/ 9781108854702
First published online: May 2020

Stephanie C. Goodhew
The Australian National University

Author for correspondence: stephanie.goodhew@anu.edu.au

Abstract: Humans can focus their attention narrowly (e.g., to read this text) or broadly (e.g., to determine which way a large crowd of people is moving). This Element comprehensively considers attentional breadth. Section 1 introduces the concept of attentional breadth, while Section 2 considers measures of attentional breadth. In particular, this section provides a critical discussion of the types of psychometric evidence which should be sought to establish the validity of measures of attentional breadth and reviews the available evidence through this lens. Section 3 considers the visual task performance consequences of attentional breadth, including prescribing several key methodological criteria that studies that manipulate attentional breadth need to meet, as well as a discussion of relevant theories and avenues for future theoretical development. Section 4 discusses the utility of the exogenous–endogenous distinction from covert shifts of attention for understanding the performance consequences of attentional breadth. Finally, Section 5 provides concluding remarks.

Keywords: visual attention, perception, attentional breadth

ISBNs: 9781108796217 (PB), 9781108854702 (OC)
ISSNs: 2515-0502 (online), 2515-0499 (print)

Contents

1 Introduction to Attentional Breadth

For most people, vision is the primary sensory modality. Vision allows us to navigate through the world and interact with it. It is our means of driving safely through traffic, avoiding obstacles, perceiving food we want to eat, reading, and recognising the face of a loved one. But at any given moment, there is far more information available to process in visual scenes than our brain is capable of processing to the level of awareness. This means that visual attention has a fundamental triaging role to play in shaping our perception of the world, by selecting certain relevant or salient information for privileged processing, while filtering out other information.

There are many different ways in which humans can regulate their visual attention. The metaphor of a 'spotlight' of attention has been used (Posner, Snyder, & Davidson, 1980), to convey the notion of a relatively small island of the visual field that is the focus of attention at any moment in time. This implies an enhanced region of processing, to the exclusion of locations or objects. Of course, this spotlight metaphor is imperfect as a model of attention, because this privileged region does not have a sharp edge but tends to gradually decline from the central focus (Downing, 1988; Eriksen & St. James, 1986; White, Ratcliff, & Starns, 2011). This region sometimes appears to have a non-monotonic roll-off function, such that the intensity of the focus does not just gradually decrease with increasing distance from central focus, but can instead reverse in direction of change (e.g., increase/decrease) of intensity with increasing distance (Caparos & Linnell, 2010; Cutzu & Tsotsos, 2003; Mounts, 2000a, 2000b; Müller, Mollenhauer, Rösler, & Kleinschmidt, 2005), rather than having a 'hard' edge as a spotlight might suggest. However, it is a useful metaphor in that it conveys the main idea of a locus of spatial attention, that is distinct from the notion of attention being applied uniformly across the visual field.

Humans can regulate their visual attention in many ways. For example, the central focus of attention (i.e., spotlight) can be shifted (translated) across space (Petersen & Posner, 2012; Posner, 1980). This spotlight does not have to be singular but can instead be split into multiple non-contiguous locations (Müller, Malinowski, Gruber, & Hillyard, 2003). It can also take on shapes other than a circle or ellipse, such as an annulus (doughnut) shape (Bleckley, Durso, Crutchfield, Engle, & Khanna, 2003; Jefferies & Di Lollo, 2015). This Element is focussed on attentional breadth, it considers the possibility that the size of the attentional spotlight can be contracted and expanded. This process has been likened to a zoom lens of a camera, in that there is a tradeoff between the area of focus and the resolution of this focus (Eriksen & St. James, 1986). When a zoom lens is narrowly focussed, only a small region of a scene is visible in sharp detail, when it is expanded a wider field of view becomes visible but at the expense of perceptual resolution. (This model will be discussed further in Section 3). This Element will discuss the nuances of conceptualising, measuring and manipulating attentional breadth, and it will review the theoretical development that has occurred in our understanding of the consequences of maintaining a given attentional breadth (e.g., broad versus narrow) for performance on visual tasks. Finally, it will consider the utility of the distinction between exogenous and endogenous attentional orienting in relation to attentional breadth.

Given that this Element is about attentional breadth, the first question we should address is its definition. What does it mean to have a narrow versus broad focus of attention? These are non-trivial questions. Some authors offer a concrete definition of attentional breadth, such as 'the visual area in which information can be acquired within one eye fixation' (Ball, Beard, Roenker, Miller, & Griggs, 1988). Others have used definitions that are more tied to the specific stimuli used, such as the processing of global versus local elements (Dale & Arnell, 2013). Some eschew a definition altogether. Attentional breadth-related concepts go by many different names in the literature, including attentional spotlight, attentional scale, attentional scope, attentional spread, attentional window, attended region size, useful field of view, and global versus local bias (Balz & Hock, 1997; Bulakowski, Bressler, & Whitney, 2007; Chong & Treisman, 2005; Dale & Arnell, 2015; Edwards, Fausto, Tetlow, Corona, & Valdes, 2018; Fang et al., 2017; Fang, Sanchez-Lopez, & Koster, 2018; Goodhew & Edwards, 2016; Goodhew, Shen, & Edwards, 2016; Heitz & Engle, 2007; Huttermann, Memmert, & Simons, 2014; Kosslyn, Brown, & Dror, 1999; Lawrence, Edwards, & Goodhew, 2020). Here, at the outset, all of these will be treated as belonging to the broad umbrella term of attentional breadth. As will become apparent in the discussion in Section 2, there are likely at least several important sub-processes or subtypes of attentional breadth. However, I will allow this to emerge organically from the review, rather than pre-empt them with strict definitions. For now, the working definition will be that attentional breadth refers to the spatial extent of the area over which spatial attention is applied, with the assumption that the area is contiguous and approximately elliptical. Throughout this Element, I will refer to manipulations that induce small (or narrow) versus large (or broad) attentional breadths. To clarify, by using these terms, I am not invoking absolute categories, but instead referring to relative sizes along a continuum of attentional breadth. That is, the effect of a given attentional breadth can only be compared with that of other attentional breadths, there is no reason to favour the notion of an absolute value of a large versus a small one.

Of course, another fundamental and important question is, why attentional breadth? Why is this Element devoted to this issue? When considering the attention literature, there is a larger amount of literature on shifts of attention, including the factors that regulate them, and their performance consequences for visual tasks, compared with that for attentional breadth. Attentional breadth is critically important. This is because the size of the attentional breadth can alter even what would be typically considered fundamental visual processes, such as our spatial or temporal acuity (Lawrence, Edwards, & Goodhew, 2020; Mounts & Edwards, 2017). That is, adopting a narrow attentional breadth can improve the level of fine spatial detail that we can resolve, such as detecting the presence of a small spatial gap in a ring. Adjusting the size of the attentional breadth can improve visual processes including those invoked in the opening of this section, such as recognising a person's face (Gao, Flevaris, Robertson, & Bentin, 2011). In addition, broadened attentional breadth has been found to be related to important functional outcomes such as drivers' crash risk (Ball, Owsley, Sloane, Roenker, & Bruni, 1993; Wood, Chaparro, Lacherez, & Hickson, 2012) and the breadth-of-attention is said to reflect a person's emotional and motivational state (Fredrickson & Branigan, 2005; Gable & Harmon-Jones, 2010a) and even regulate mood (Gu, Yang, Li, Zhou, & Gao, 2017). Finally, different measures of attentional breadth have been found to vary as a function of different individual characteristics, such as age, personality, and working memory capacity (Kreitz, Furley, Memmert, & Simons, 2015; Lawrence, Edwards, & Goodhew, 2018; Wilson, Lowe, Ruppel, Pratt, & Ferber, 2016). It is, therefore, clearly important for us to understand this process, from both a theoretical and a practical perspective.

This Element is timely because the field is at a critical juncture. That is, the field has amassed sufficient evidence to highlight how greater clarity and consensus is required in both the operationalisation and conceptualisation of attentional breadth if the field is to advance. The goal of this Element is to provide a discussion and a framework to guide this process forward.

2 Measuring Attentional Breadth

In this section, I will discuss some of the most commonly used methods designed to measure attentional breadth. In doing so, I will highlight where there are alternative attentional processes that could underlie performance on these tasks, to determine whether they are truly gauging attentional breadth or potentially some other attentional or cognitive process. I will also consider the potential underlying structure of attentional breadth. That is, attentional breadth may not be a monolithic construct. Take, for analogy, working memory. Working memory is an important construct, but it has multiple meaningful subcomponents, such as a central executive, visuospatial sketchpad, and phonological loop (Baddeley, 2012; Baddeley & Hitch, 1974). In the domain of attention, Corbetta and Shulman (2002) differentiate between top-down attentional processes that serve functions including goal execution and action selection, and more bottom-up mechanisms driven by stimulus salience. It is possible, probable even, that attentional breadth may have a multifaceted underlying structure of subcomponents. If true, then this should be revealed via convergent and divergent patterns of associations, in individuals' performance on these tasks. This would be determined by having the same group of individuals perform each of these tasks, and examining the correlation between them (e.g., if individual X is gauged to have a broad attentional breadth on task A and individual Y a narrow breadth on task A, then convergent evidence for tasks A and B would be if individual X was also gauged to have a broad attentional breadth on task B and individual Y a narrow one). That is, theoretically, if attentional breadth is a construct that actually does underlie performance on all of these different tasks, then performance on them should be correlated. In contrast, if there are meaningful distinctions between the different aspects of attentional breadth, then performance on particular types of tasks may diverge from others. For example, while all measures of attentional breadth should have some relationship with one another, if two tasks gauge the same subcomponent of attentional breadth, then their correlation should be higher than either of their correlations with the measure of a different subcomponent of attentional breadth. Other additional types of evidence will be discussed later in this section. Considering alternative explanations for performance on tasks thought to measure attentional breadth is important. If a task does not measure what it claims to, then this could lead to a wrongful conclusion regarding the true structure of attentional breadth. Following the introduction of each of these methods, I will introduce some key criteria to consider in the search for validating evidence for measures of attentional breadth. Then, I will critically discuss the evidence regarding whether or not they do all indeed reflect attentional breadth, and the same aspect of it. However, the available evidence is limited and incomplete, therefore, I will make recommendations regarding the steps that are required in future research to ensure that we have a solid foundation from which to study and understand attentional breadth and its potentially multifaceted nature.

2.1 Navon

Navon stimuli are compound stimuli, in which information can be presented independently to participants at both a global and a local level (see Figure 1

SSSSS
S
S
S
S

Figure 1 An example illustration of a Navon stimulus. Here, the global letter is
'T', whereas the local elements are the letter 'S' (note that all figures are
intended for the purposes of illustration and are not necessarily to scale).

for an example). The original study (Navon, 1977) used letter stimuli,
whereby a larger letter (global level) was made up of multiple occurrences
of the same small letter (local level). These stimuli were introduced with the
aim of studying the stages of visual scene analysis (Navon, 1977, 1981). It
was found that information at the global level was processed and affected
performance even when participants were instructed to attend to the local
level, whereas the reverse did not occur. The local level did not interfere with
the processing of the global level content (Navon, 1977). This led to the
conclusion that global processing was completed before local processing,
called the 'global precedence' (Navon, 1981). Metaphorically, this means
that participants are inclined to see the *forest* before the *trees*. The relative
advantage for processing the global relative to the local elements of such
stimuli is one that has persisted through decades of research (Badcock,
Whitworth, Badcock, & Lovegrove, 1990; Baumann & Kuhl, 2005; Hoar &
Linnell, 2013; Navon, 1977, 1981).

It should be noted that the concept of global precedence has been challenged
(Kinchla & Wolfe, 1979) and that whether or not a processing advantage for the
global elements of such stimuli is observed does depend on a number of factors,
including the respective sizes of the global and local elements, and how densely
the local elements are arranged (Goodhew & Plummer, 2019; Kimchi & Palmer,
1982; Pomerantz, 1983; Yovel, Levy, & Yovel, 2001). Indeed, under certain
conditions, a bias in favour of *local* processing can be obtained (Kinchla &
Wolfe, 1979). In addition, it has been found that such stimulus parameters have
a greater effect on the visual search for global targets than for local targets (Enns
& Kingstone, 1995). However, more recent work has supported Navon's fundamental idea of visual processing progressing from a broad brushstroke initial

sweep, followed by the more detailed processing of individual elements (Bar et al., 2006; Greene & Oliva, 2009).

Since their introduction, Navon stimuli have been developed as measures of attentional breadth. There are two main types of tasks where Navon stimuli are used (hereafter, 'Navon tasks' or 'versions of Navon task'). Here, I will refer to them as the *directed* and *undirected* versions of the Navon task. The latter is sometimes called the *divided attention* Navon task, however, I think it is preferable to make as few assumptions as possible about the particular attentional processes that are occurring when naming tasks without evidence to support this. Instead, the directed versus undirected distinction refers to the task instructions and does not make assumptions about whether attention is divided, or instead rapidly switches between the different levels. In the directed Navon task, participants' attention is directed to a particular level of the stimulus using direct task instructions. For example, participants are instructed to identify the letter presented at the global level for a block of trials. At the (task-irrelevant) local level, stimuli that are congruent versus incongruent with the target stimuli at the global level are presented, and participants' response efficiency[1] to identify the global target is compared for the congruent versus incongruent trials. In another block of trials, participants would be instructed to identify the letter presented at the local level, and their relative performance in doing so when congruent versus incongruent information is presented at the global level is gauged. If the interference from the incongruent (relative to the congruent) trials is greater when the target level is at the local level, then this is said to show a global advantage and, therefore, a broad attentional breadth, whereas if interference from the incongruent trials is greater when the target level is the global level, then this is said to show a local advantage and, therefore, a narrow attentional breadth (Caparos, Linnell, Bremner, de Fockert, & Davidoff, 2013; Dale & Arnell, 2013; Navon, 1977).

In contrast, in the undirected version of the Navon task, participants are not instructed to identify the letters at a prescribed level. Instead, they are instructed to identify one of a prescribed set of targets (e.g., the letter 'T' or 'H'). One and only one of these targets appear in each Navon stimulus, and the target can occur at either the global or local level. Participants are simply asked to identify which target stimulus is present, as quickly and as accurately as possible, irrespective

---

[1] For such tasks, by design accuracy is typically at or near maximum (i.e., ceiling). Accuracy is measured to ensure the participants' ability and willingness to comply with task instructions, and to check for speed-accuracy tradeoffs. In such designs, response speed is the primary dependent variable. I use the term 'response efficiency' or 'response speed' to refer to faster responses, assuming equally accurate or more accurate responses in this condition relative to the slower condition.

of which level it appears. Here, the relative response efficiency to the targets at the global versus local level provides an index of attentional breadth. If responses are facilitated for the global relative to the local level, then this is used to infer a relatively broad attentional breadth, whereas if responses are facilitated for the local versus the global level, then this leads to an inference of a relatively narrow attentional breadth (Gable & Harmon-Jones, 2008; Goodhew & Plummer, 2019; McKone et al., 2010). The most common instantiation of the undirected Navon task is to have the target appearing equally often at each level over the block of trials, and trial types are randomly intermixed.

The Navon task has been adapted to measure *attentional resizing efficiency*, which is an important attentional function. This is because different perceptual and cognitive processes benefit from different attentional breadths. For example, if one is trying to resolve final spatial detail in order to read text, then this perceptual process would benefit from a relatively narrow attentional breadth, and correspondingly be compromised by a broad attentional breadth (Balz & Hock, 1997; Lawrence, Edwards, & Goodhew, 2020). In contrast, if one is scanning a crowd to locate a friend, then this would likely benefit from a broader attentional breadth and would be relatively impaired with a narrower attentional breadth (Gao et al., 2011; Macrae & Lewis, 2002). While in the laboratory we typically study the impact of attentional breadth on one process at a time, in real-world vision, humans are often juggling and rapidly switching between multiple tasks with different demands. For example, when driving a car, reading the speedometer requires a narrow focus of spatial attention, in order to resolve the fine spatial information and avoid interference from surrounding instruments, whereas monitoring the road for any change or movement (e.g., a child approaching the road, or the trajectories of other cars) requires a broad focus. Similarly, when meeting up with a friend, one may have to switch between a narrow focus for reading a text message and a broad focus for identifying the friend's face in a crowd, or identifying what direction the bulk of the crowd is moving in. The laboratory research tells us that optimising attention to facilitate these processes requires adopting different attentional breadths. These functional requirements of real-world vision demand that humans can efficiently change between one attentional breadth and another. In other words, they can rapidly and dynamically *resize* their attentional breadth.

Some early literature examined attentional breadth resizing via what was dubbed 'level readiness'. Ward (1982) found that when participants were directed to identify the information at different levels (global/local) of Navon stimuli, they were quicker to do this if the previous trial had required the response at the same level compared with a response about the previous level. Other studies have observed similar results (Robertson, Egly, Lamb, & Kerth,

1993; Wilkinson, Halligan, Marshall, Büchel, & Dolan, 2001). This effect has been observed when the stimulus changes location, colour, polarity, or contrast between trials, and it can persist for up to three *seconds* between one trial and the next (Robertson, 1996). Some work has suggested that even providing participants with a cue about the nature of the upcoming stimulus does not allow them to recover from the deleterious effect of an opposite-level preceding trial (Hubner, 2000), whereas other work has suggested that this may produce a benefit (Stoffer, 1993).

More recent research has quantified attentional resizing costs by changing the proportion of trials where the target appears at different levels (e.g., target present at the global level 80 per cent of the time and at the local level 20 per cent of the time, and vice versa in a different block). This is designed to set attentional breadth at the level at which the target most often appears, and then the time to cost of resizing attention to the other level for the minority of trials can be gauged (Calcott & Berkman, 2014; Goodhew & Plummer, 2019). Using this method, average resizing costs around 100–150 ms have been observed, although with marked individual differences, such that resizing takes some individuals almost no time at all, and some individuals take up to 400–500 ms (Goodhew & Plummer, 2019) which is in the ballpark of the duration of other noteworthy deficits such as the attentional blink (Dell'Acqua et al., 2015; Raymond, Shapiro, & Arnell, 1992).

One suggestion has been that Navon stimuli induce changes in 'categorical' attention, rather than attentional breadth per se. That is, when participants attend to the global versus local elements of the stimuli, rather than this being mediated by changes in attentional breadth, participants may be essentially adopting attentional sets for *small, local elements* versus *large, global elements*, with their attention spread over equivalent spatial extents in both cases (Robertson et al., 1993). For a similar notion, see Coren, Ward, and Enns (2004). This is an interesting possibility to consider. However, one reason to doubt such a claim is that attending to the global versus local elements of Navon stimuli have been found to induce different attentional breadths, as revealed by functional magnetic resonance imaging (fMRI). Sasaki et al. (2001) used fMRI to measure activation in occipital areas in response to global and local (Navon) stimuli. Participants were instructed to either attend to or passively view hierarchical stimuli, and in the attend condition, participants were required to perform a shape identification task. Accuracy in this task was high. Sasaki et al. (2001) found that attending to the global stimuli activated more peripheral regions than for local stimuli and that the magnitude of activation for the local attention condition over the same area was greater than for the global attention condition, which is consistent with the concept of a zoom lens. This was definitely true in a number of extrastriate areas but was also true in the primary visual cortex (V1) for some participants. This is consistent with the zoom-lens model of attention (discussed in Section 3). More broadly, this is consistent with the notion of attentional breadth being implicated in identifying local versus global Navon targets, such that the spatial extent of the area over which attentional resources are spread changes according to whether participants attend to the global or local levels. This is good convergent evidence that behavioural-based Navon effects (e.g., faster responses at the global level) do likely reflect the adoption of a corresponding (e.g., broad) attentional breadth.

2.2 Kimchi and Palmer

Kimchi and Palmer stimuli have also been proposed to operationalise attentional breadth (Basso, Schefft, Ris, & Dember, 1996; Behrmann et al., 2006; Fredrickson & Branigan, 2005; Gasper & Clore, 2002; Kimchi & Palmer, 1982; Koldewyn, Jiang, Weigelt, & Kanwisher, 2013; Kramer, Ellenberg, Leonard, & Share, 1996; Pletzer, Scheuringer, & Scherndl, 2017). Typically, these stimuli are used in a task whereby participants are presented with a standard shape configuration (e.g., four smaller squares arranged in the shape of a square), and then with two other comparison configurations to choose from with respect to which the participant considers the most similar to the standard shape (see Figure 2). Of the two comparison options, one is consistent with the standard shape at the global level (e.g., a global square but local triangles), while the other is consistent with the standard shape at the local level (e.g., local squares but global triangle). This means that which of the two available options a participant chooses is thought to indicate whether their attention was directed to the global or the local level of the test stimulus and, therefore, whether they had a broad or narrow attentional breadth.

One potential downside with using the Kimchi and Palmer stimuli in this way is that given the nature of the task, it is typically only practical to ask participants to make such judgements about a relatively small number of stimulus configurations (e.g., 1–8). This means that the resulting measure is relatively coarse (e.g., a scale of 1–8 for how often they selected the globally-similar stimulus). However, even with this, performance on tasks using Kimchi and Palmer's stimuli are reliably associated with meaningful variance in other psychological processes (Basso et al., 1996; Dale & Arnell, 2015; Koldewyn et al., 2013). Performance-based measures of visual search have also been developed using these stimuli (Enns & Kingstone, 1995), which circumvent such issues.

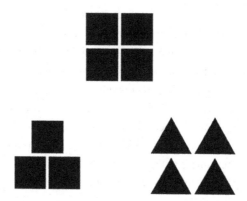

Figure 2 An example illustration of Kimchi and Palmer type stimuli. The top stimulus is a global square made up of local level squares. The bottom left stimulus (a triangle made up of squares) shares the same local elements as the top stimulus, but has a conflicting global configuration, whereas the bottom right stimulus (a square made up of triangles) has the same global configuration as the top stimulus, but conflicting local elements. Participants could be asked to indicate which of the two bottom stimuli they think looks most like the top stimulus.

2.3 Flanker

The flanker task is where a stimulus is presented, with surrounding task-irrelevant flanker stimuli (see Figure 3). For example, in the centre of the screen, the target letter 'E' could be presented, and the participants' task is to identify whether the letter 'E' or 'F' is presented. One letter could appear to the left of the target and one letter could appear to the right of the target. These two flanking letters would be the same letter as one another, but crucially, they are either congruent (E E E) or incongruent (F E F) with respect to the target[2]. The flanker effect is defined as a slower response to the target when the flankers are incongruent, relative to when they are congruent (Biggs & Gibson, 2018; Eriksen & Eriksen, 1974; Richard, Lee, & Vecera, 2008). The spatial separation between the target and flankers can be varied, and the flanker effect typically diminishes as this separation increases (Eriksen & Eriksen, 1974).

The flanker effect is often classified as a measure of executive control of attention (Fan, McCandliss, Fossella, Flombaum, & Posner, 2005; Hotton,

---

[2] Note that congruency does not necessarily imply that the target and flankers have to be identical. For example, they can be not identical but be associated with the same (congruent) or different (incongruent) response. However, in contemporary work, this is one of the most common ways that congruency is operationalised: same identity flankers as the target (congruent) versus different identity flankers compared with the target (incongruent).

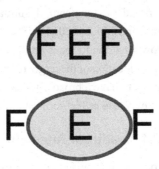

Figure 3 An example illustration of an incongruent flanker display at two different spatial separations (e.g., the top panel at a close target–flanker separation, and bottom panel at a further target–flanker separation). It is incongruent because the identity of the flankers (F) conflicts with the identity of the target (E). The participants' task could be E/F discrimination of the central letter. Ellipses with outlines indicate hypothetical attentional breadth. In the top panel, the flankers are included in the attentional breadth and, therefore, should produce a robust flanker effect. In contrast, in the bottom panel, the flankers fall outside of the attentional breadth and, therefore, should produce minimal to no flanker effect. In this way, the magnitude of the flanker effect at different spatial separations is thought to provide a gauge of attentional breadth.

Derakshan, & Fox, 2018; Moriya, 2018; Najmi, Hindash, & Amir, 2010; Posner & Rothbart, 2007). As an extension of this, the flanker effect has also been conceptualised as a measure of attentional breadth. The logic here is that the presence of the flanker effect is predicated on the flankers falling within one's attentional breadth. Gauging flanker effects at different target–flanker separations can provide insight into how broad attention is spread (Biggs & Gibson, 2018; Heitz & Engle, 2007; Lavie, 1995; Rowe, Hirsh, & Anderson, 2007). For example, if in one condition a flanker effect is observed at a near but not far target–flanker separation, then this is said to reflect a narrower attentional breadth than another condition where a flanker effect is observed at both near and far separations. For a useful summary of the various attentional measures that can be derived from a flanker task, see Enns and Akhtar (1989).

When the target always appears in the same location (e.g., the centre of the screen), then the patterns of performance probably reflect one's *minimum* attentional breadth. This is because, in this scenario, it is always adaptive to have a narrow attentional breadth, because it is only ever the target that requires explicit identification, and the flankers are always task-irrelevant (although for an alternative argument based on the featural similarity of the target and flankers, see Buetti, Lleras, and Moore (2014)). This means that an adaptive strategy would be to narrow attention to focus on the target to the exclusion of the flankers. In contrast, if the location of the target is unpredictable from trial-to-trial, then it may be adaptive to have a broader focus at the start of the trial. In this case, the flanker effect may also reflect some attentional resizing processes.

2.4 Breadth-of-Attention

The breadth-of-attention paradigm entails the brief presentation of two clusters of shapes presented equidistant from fixation, and the participants' task is to report information about both clusters (see Figure 4). The idea here is that when a minimum criterion of accuracy is maintained at this task with stimuli a given distance from fixation, then this provides a measure of attentional breadth (Huttermann, Bock, & Memmert, 2012; Huttermann & Memmert, 2015; Huttermann et al., 2014). For earlier versions of this task, see Enns and Girgus (1985), and Pomerantz and Schwaitzberg (1975). In this way, the breadth-of-attention task can be thought of as providing a measure of *maximum* attentional breadth. For example, several degrees of visual angle to the left of the centre, four adjacent but non-overlapping shapes could be presented, a combination of circles and squares, where each individual shape can be either light or dark grey. The same type of stimulus (but with different combinations of shapes and colours) is presented the same distance to the right of fixation. The participants' task is to report the number of light grey triangles (firstly in one stimulus, and then the other), and they are only deemed correct if they report the number of light grey triangles correctly for both. Over a series of trials, the distance between the stimuli along a given meridian (horizontal, vertical and diagonal) at which participants can score 75 per cent correct is considered the breadth of their attention (Huttermann et al., 2014). The breadth-of-attention

  •

Figure 4 An example illustration of the breadth-of-attention task. Stimuli are presented briefly. The participants' task could be to report the number of light grey triangles in the stimulus on the left, followed by the stimulus on the right (e.g., two responses). The distance between the centre of the screen and the location of the shapes is varied to gauge the breadth-of-attention.

task has been found to reveal an elliptical shape attended region (Huttermann et al., 2014).

Breadth of attention, as gauged by this task, has been found to differentiate between individuals of different ages (Huttermann et al., 2012), those with athletic expertise versus those without (and even different shape breadths for 'horizontal' sports such as soccer versus 'vertical' sports such as volleyball or basketball) (Huttermann et al., 2014), and individuals in different motivational and mood states (Huttermann & Memmert, 2015). This means that it clearly captures meaningful variance. Whether it is attentional breadth or another cognitive or attentional process remains to be conclusively demonstrated. This is because, as the proponents of this metric of attentional breadth themselves acknowledge, it is not possible to rule out the role of other attentional processes, including the rapid shift of attention between the two sets of stimuli (Huttermann et al., 2014), and even attentional splitting. Humans can allocate their attention to non-contiguous locations (Müller et al., 2003), and, therefore, it is possible that in the breadth-of-attention paradigm, they manage to split rather than spread their attention to perform the task.

2.5 Useful Field of View

The useful field of view (UFOV) task has been proposed as a measure of 'useful vision', which is defined as the visual area in which information can be acquired within one eye fixation (Ball et al., 1988; Sekuler & Ball, 1986). This has since been classified as a measure of attentional breadth (Kreitz et al., 2015). There have been a few different variants of the core UFOV task, but the essence of all those that are said to reflect attention is that participants juggle two tasks concurrently. One task involves making a response about a centrally presented and fixated stimulus, whereas the other involves making a response (e.g., identity, location) regarding a peripherally presented object. This can be in the presence or absence of distractors, to gauge what is called 'selective attention' or 'divided attention' respectively (Ball et al., 1988; Cosman, Lees, Lee, Rizzo, & Vecera, 2012; Kreitz et al., 2015) (see Figure 5).

In some of the early versions of the task, the stimuli consisted of one schematic face presented in the centre of the screen, and then in the periphery appeared multiple outline boxes of the same size and luminance as the central face presented along eight meridians (i.e., along the cardinal and oblique axes). On key trials, a (face) stimulus appeared in the periphery, and the participants' task was to localise it. The difficulty of the concurrent central task can be varied (e.g., face detection, versus facial expression identification) (Ball et al., 1988; Sekuler & Ball, 1986). Performance in these dual-task conditions can be compared with performance under

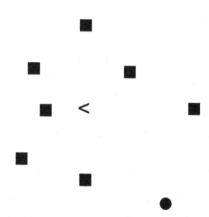

Figure 5 An example illustration of a useful field of view (UFOV) task. Here, the tasks could be to (a) identify whether the central arrow is pointing left versus right, or (b) to identify the location of the peripheral circle stimulus.

single-task conditions (e.g., just localisation task alone) to confirm that any deficits do not arise from general poor vision, such as loss of peripheral acuity (Sekuler & Ball, 1986). More recent work has tested the UFOV with more complex stimuli, such as driving scenes (Seya, Nakayasu, & Yagi, 2013).

Early work with the UFOV task found that older adults performed worse than younger adults (Ball et al., 1988; Sekuler & Ball, 1986). Furthermore, Ball et al. (1993) conducted a retrospective analysis of older drivers with varying frequencies of crashes (state recorded) over the past five years. These authors then assessed a variety of variables, including UFOV, to determine their predictive validity in relation to crash risk. It was found that UFOV had the strongest relationship with, and was the single best predictor of crash frequency, even over and above participants' chronological age within the older adult cohort. In addition, it has been found that practice on the UFOV improves performance in this task (Sekuler & Ball, 1986). However, with sufficient practice, participants will show improvement on virtually any visual or cognitive task. A more rigorous test of a training benefit is to show that training results in a transfer to another unpractised task that gauges the same underlying process. In this vein, more recent work has shown that UFOV training generalises to improved driving performance, and these gains were even maintained 18 months after training (Roenker, Cissell, Ball, Wadley, & Edwards, 2003). While clearly important from a practical perspective, it is unclear from a theoretical perspective whether *attentional breadth*, in particular, mediates these changes, or whether these changes may relate to other cognitive processes such as the speed of processing (Edwards et al., 2018).

2.6 Spatial Distribution of Inhibition of Return

The spatial distribution of inhibition of return (IOR) involves the presentation of simple cue stimulus (e.g., an outline disc) followed by a to be detected target stimulus (e.g., a disc) that can appear at the same or one of many different locations relative to the cue. Attentional breadth is gauged by measuring how the effect of the cue generalises over the spatial separation between the cue and the target (see Figure 6). More specifically, IOR is the phenomenon whereby following the presentation of cue, the benefit of the cue (in terms of response speed for subsequent target stimuli at the cued location) can turn into an impairment at longer cue–target intervals (Klein, 2000; Posner & Cohen, 1984). This is thought to occur because when a cue initially shifts attention to the cued location, attention is said to disengage from this location when a target does not follow soon after. IOR is typically strongest when the cue and subsequent target occupy the same spatial location, however, it also occurs at non-zero spatial separations between the cue and target. It is thought that the cue and the target need to fall within the same attentional window for IOR to occur

A.

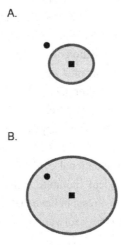

B.

Figure 6 An example illustration of the logic of the spatial distribution of IOR measure of attentional breadth. The black square is the cue, which appears prior to the black circle target. Ellipses with outlines indicate hypothetical attentional breadths. In (a), the narrow attentional breadth around the cue excludes the target and, therefore, minimal or no IOR would be expected here. In contrast, in (b), the broad attentional breadth around the cue includes the target and, therefore, IOR would be expected here. This shows how the strength of IOR at different spatial separations between the cue and target can be used as a measure of attentional breadth.

and, therefore, the spatial gradient over which this effect occurs has been adapted into a measure of attentional breadth (Bennett & Pratt, 2001). When the effect of IOR diminishes rapidly with increasing spatial separation between the cue and target, then this is used to infer a relatively narrow breadth of attention. In contrast, when the effect of IOR diminishes slowly with this increasing spatial separation, then this leads to the inference of a relatively broad breadth of attention (Bennett & Pratt, 2001; Lawrence et al., 2018; Wilson et al., 2016). In addition, this measure can be conceptualised as a measure of attentional preference because the task does not specifically compel a particular attentional breadth. Furthermore, it is also important not to use placeholder stimuli, because these can unduly constrain the measure (Lawrence et al., 2018; Taylor, Chan, Bennett, & Pratt, 2015).

2.7 The Operationalisation of Attentional Breadth and Its Potential Components

Operationalisation refers to a set of stimuli and task parameters and the resulting measures that are designed to reflect a hypothesised psychological process. A crucially important question is how *valid* this operationalisation is. In other words, does it truly capture the intended psychological process? We can never directly observe any covert attentional processes, including attentional breadth. Instead, we rely on the careful selection of stimuli, tasks and outcome measures in the service of providing insight into what we believe to be the underlying attentional mechanism or process. For good science, this selection process must be guided by evidence, not (just) intuition. For example, we cannot use the undirected Navon task simply because it appears, on the face of it, like it *ought* to reflect attentional breadth. Instead, we need foundational evidence to support this assertion. Such crucial foundational evidence can be surprisingly slow to enter the cognitive–psychological literature, relative to the prevalence and popularity of the use of the measures. I believe that this needs to be an important part of research if our field is to move forward in the most meaningful way that it could.

To recap, some of these tasks, the UFOV in particular, are clearly related to crucial practical outcomes such as driving performance (Ball et al., 1993; Roenker et al., 2003). Similarly, it has been claimed that regular broadening of attention can alleviate psychological distress (Gu et al., 2017). However, here a *theoretical* lens is adopted, which considers the question: what psychological process underlies such changes? Is it attentional breadth? Only attentional breadth? Or attentional breadth in concert with other processes? What aspect of attentional breadth? Here the goal is to answer such questions. In the first instance, the primary goal is to understand *why* people perform the way that they do. Considering *how* to use this knowledge to leverage desired outcomes (such as improving driving performance) will naturally follow as a logical next step.

In comparison, it is interesting that in other areas of psychology, such as those that rely heavily on questionnaires, the issue of operationalisation and its validity is more central. For example, if one were to propose a new measure of anxiety, it would not be considered sufficient to highlight that the items on it appears to capture what we think that psychological construct is. Instead, before a new measure could be introduced, it would need to undergo reliability and validity assessment, including showing that it did correlate with things that it should and did not correlate with others that it ought not to. I believe that cognitive psychology could benefit from stricter psychometric criteria for its measures. In the sections 2.7.1–2.7.6, I highlight such psychometric principles and criteria to take into consideration in relation to the operationalisation of attentional breadth.

2.7.1 The Potential Structure of Attentional Breadth

The previous sections (2.1–2.6) highlighted how a diverse array of different stimuli and tasks are used to measure what is broadly considered the same construct: *attentional breadth*. There are, of course, additional paradigms in the same vein, but here the focus has been on some common ones. Even within these, there are a number of at least superficially quite large differences. For example, some claim to gauge attentional breadth by responses to a single level of sole compound stimulus presented on each trial (e.g., Navon), whereas others claim to gauge attentional breadth by responses to a myriad of peripherally presented stimuli when participants are engaged in another task (e.g., UFOV). This raises some important questions, do they all measure the same underlying construct? Should they? Whether they should or not boils down to what the theorised structure of attentional breadth is. As highlighted previously, working memory is an important construct that has meaningful divisions or sub-processes, and it is possible, probable even, that attentional breadth does too. To my knowledge, to date, there are no theoretical models of attentional breadth that propose and validate such a structure. However, as will become apparent when I review the existing literature on the validity of attentional measurement, there do appear to be some important distinctions, such as between those that measure attentional breadth *preference*, and those that measure attentional breadth *control*-related functions, such as the ability to adopt a prescribed attentional breadth. There may be additional distinctions still. When assessing the validity of attentional breadth measures, the hypothesised underlying structure needs to be taken into consideration.

Indeed, many psychological processes are not monolithic but instead consist of meaningful sub-processes. For example, *depression, anxiety,* and *stress* all belong to the broader construct of *negative affect*. The Depression Anxiety and Stress Scale (DASS) measures each of these processes separately using subscales for each process, but these three subscales can also be combined to provide an aggregate measure of the overarching construct of negative affect (Lovibond & Lovibond, 1995; Onie & Most, 2017). Because the subscales for depression, anxiety, and stress are all measures of negative affect, they ought to correlate with one another, and they do (Lovibond & Lovibond, 1995). Any individual subscale that seeks to measure depression, ought to have higher correlations with other measures of depression (e.g., the Beck Depression Inventory), than measures of anxiety (e.g., the Beck Anxiety Inventory), and vice versa for anxiety. This pattern of results was established in early psychometric testing of the DASS (Lovibond & Lovibond, 1995). In addition, factor analysis applied to all of the questionnaire items was found to support the three-factor structure in both clinical and non-clinical samples (Brown, Chorpita, Korotitsch, & Barlow, 1997; Lovibond & Lovibond, 1995).

Assessing the validity of attentional breadth measures means searching for these sorts of convergent and divergent associations among hypothesised sub-processes. While there is a paucity of theoretical models to base this on, let us say for the sake of argument that attentional breadth is found to consist of two major distinct but interrelated components: attentional breadth *control*, such as the ability to set a prescribed attentional breadth, and the range of attentional breadths that a person is capable of instantiating (i.e., maximum minus minimum attentional breadth) on the one hand, and attentional breadth *preference* (i.e., the tendency to adopt a given attentional breadth in the absence of compelling task demands) on the other. With this structure, individuals' performance on Control Measure A should be more highly correlated with their performance on Control Measure B, than it is with either Preference Measure C or Preference Measure D, which also ought to have higher correlations with one another than cross-correlations with the two control measures. While such patterns of correlations would provide preliminary evidence for such a proposed model of attentional breadth, further supporting evidence could arise from factor analytic procedures. If a group of individuals complete a battery of purported attentional breadth measures, factor analysis is designed to provide insight into the underlying factor structure and how the items (in this case, experimental measures) coalesce onto these factors. If there are three distinct attentional breadth factors, then evidence for these should emerge from factor analysis. The analysis would also provide important information regarding what different attentional breadth measures relate most strongly to which of these factors.

It should be noted that one study attempted a factor analysis on measures of attentional breadth (Milne & Szczerbinski, 2009). However, the measures selected were predominately drawn from the autism literature and had little overlap with the attentional breadth measures described here (the only one of the previously described methods included was the directed Navon). The authors failed to find evidence for any unitary underlying factor of attentional breadth, in fact, the fourteen attentional breadth tasks loaded onto seven different factors, indicating that diversity rather than unity dominated. Clearly, there is more work to be done on the measurement and conceptualisation of attentional breadth. This work will need to consider the potential sub-processes of attentional breadth.

In section 2.7.2, I discuss the nuanced issue of measurement reliability, and I identify three criteria that I believe future research should consider in attentional breadth measure and model validity assessment. Some of these are the types of evidence researchers have already sought (e.g., correlations between different measures), and some are more novel. In addition, I explain the considerable methodological challenges that the search for this type of evidence needs to tackle if the right conclusions are to be reached. In essence, this should provide researchers will a useful roadmap for navigating some of the complexities of this type of science.

2.7.2 Reliability

When assessing convergent and divergent associations among different measures, some form of correlation is required (even more sophisticated approaches such as multiple regression still encounter the same fundamental issue). However, any observed correlation between two given measures is constrained by the *reliability* of the measures entering into the correlation. If an unreliable measure or measures are used, then the wrong conclusions could be reached about the true nature of the underlying relationships. Reliability, when it comes to assessing correlations amounts to: how consistently does the measure rank-order individuals? That is, is the position of individuals in the distribution scores preserved across time and different administrations of the same test (test-retest reliability), or even from the first to the second half of trials (split-half reliability)[3]? For example, if one individual is gauged to have a broad attentional breadth based on the first half of the trials, would they also be classified as

---

[3] More sophisticated measures can answer questions regarding whether an individual is likely to receive precisely the same absolute score, not just the same relative position in the distribution (which could entail a mean shift for all in the distribution). However, if a measure cannot even preserve the relative position of individuals, it is unlikely to be able to preserve their absolute scores.

having a broad attentional breadth on the second half of the trials? Crucially, this is different from the reliability with which a measure will demonstrate an effect averaged across individuals. For example, it is distinct from the reliability of the measure in showing a group level global precedence effect when averaged across all of the individuals in the sample (Hedge, Powell, & Sumner, 2018). In fact, seminal recent work has shown that these two types of reliability are in intrinsic conflict (Hedge et al., 2018). For example, the flanker effect is highly reliable at the group level, in that most or all individuals are susceptible to it and it is robustly observed over a group of participants. However, as a direct consequence of this reduced between participant variance, it can have poor reliability when it comes to rank-ordering individuals, the type of reliability that is important for correlations (Goodhew & Edwards, 2019; Hedge et al., 2018).

Different versions or adaptations of the same basic paradigm can have different levels of reliability, therefore, it does not necessarily mean that the flanker can never be used in correlational research. However, the standard version (Hedge et al., 2018) at present would be inappropriate to do so, because it would unduly constrain any observed correlation with other constructs. More broadly, this issue of reliability is one that needs to be confronted when tackling the issue of validity assessment for measures of attentional breadth. Otherwise, the wrong conclusion may be reached. This is because if a measure is not reliable in its ranking of individuals, then this will constrain the maximum observable correlation between this and any other variable (Spearman, 1910). This means that a measure with low reliability could lead to a null observed correlation, even if this does not reflect the true state of affairs. For example, if a measure of attentional breadth has low reliability, this could lead to a null correlation between working memory and attentional breadth, even if the aspect of attentional breadth it is designed to measure is actually associated with working memory (for an in-depth discussion of these issues, see Goodhew and Edwards (2019)). This means that the reliability of measurement is a crucial consideration in relation to understanding measures of attentional breadth.

In addition, it is worth bearing in mind that this concept of reliability assumes that the underlying construct is stable. That is, if a construct such as attentional breadth preference is relatively stable, like personality or trait anxiety, then measures of attentional breadth preference should be stable over time for any given individual. However, if attentional breadth preference varies across time (more like mood or state anxiety), then one would not necessarily expect the same individual to receive the same attentional breadth preference measure at all measured time points. This means that the psychometric properties of the measure would need to be assessed in other ways, or on shorter timescales.

Another attentional literature has grappled with this issue of explaining stable variance from a dynamic attentional process. This literature relates to different individuals' tendency to respond differently to different types of stimuli. That is, individuals with high levels of anxiety are more likely to allocate their attention to a threatening stimulus than to a neutral stimulus (Bar-Haim, Lamy, Pergamin, Bakermans-Kranenburg, & van Ijzendoorn, 2007; MacLeod, Mathews, & Tata, 1986). A meta-analysis showed that this effect was reliable for those with high levels of anxiety, but not those with low levels of anxiety (Bar-Haim et al., 2007). This effect is not just a curiosity or side effect but instead appears to play a key maintaining and possibly aetiological role in the anxiety itself, such that treating the bias can reduce anxiety (MacLeod & Clarke, 2015). However, sometimes the measures demonstrating these effects (e.g., dot-probe) have been criticised as having low reliability. (When considering this, it is important not to confuse mean group level effect replicability with reliability in gauging an individuals' attentional bias). But if we consider it from the perspective of individual differences reliability, attention is dynamic, not static. The location to which an individual is attending or the type of stimulus which holds sway over their attention may change over time. Indeed, in a recent review authored by leaders in this field, the attentional bias effect was described as 'probabilistic' (MacLeod, Grafton, & Notebaert, 2019). Consistent with this, the bias itself can be moderated by factors such as an individuals' level of attentional control (Taylor, Cross, & Amir, 2016), or their current working memory load (Delchau, Christensen, O'Kearney, & Goodhew, 2019). Therefore, even though anxiety does appear to be meaningfully associated with an attentional bias toward threatening stimuli, it is not necessarily the case that this should be invariably expected to be observed at all times in all individuals. This, of course, creates something of a conundrum when it comes to assessing reliability.

Another branch of this literature has tackled this dynamicity head-on. Emerging literature shows that the *variability* of the attentional bias over time is strongly associated with anxiety and post-traumatic stress disorder (Cox, Christensen, & Goodhew, 2018; Iacoviello et al., 2014; Zvielli, Bernstein, & Koster, 2015). These measures are obtained by computing traditional bias scores (e.g., subtracting response times to identify a target when it appears in the same location as a neutral stimulus from when it appears in the same location as a threatening stimulus) over small trial bins (e.g., five trials), rather than all trials, and then quantifying the variability (e.g., standard deviation) of the resulting scores. Trait anxious individuals show greater variability in bias scores over time than non-anxious individuals. This means that an anxious individual may not be showing a bias toward threat at every given moment, but they are more likely to show variability over time in the extent to which they are attending to threat or not. This may reflect the temporal dynamics of competing priorities of vigilance to threat, versus avoidance from threat in anxiety (Koster, Crombez, Verschuere, Van Damme, & Wiersema, 2006; Proud, Goodhew, & Edwards, 2020). The implication of this for attentional breadth is significant: if attentional breadth is dynamic rather than static, then the field may need to adopt more innovative ways of quantifying effects than just averaging over all of the available trials at once. Measures of variability such as those discussed here offer one potential avenue forward, but others may also need to be considered.

To summarise, issues such as reliability, and even whether the underlying process ought to be static or dynamic, are important considerations when assessing the validity of attempts to operationalise attentional breadth. Reliability is considered a necessary but not sufficient condition for *validity*, which is another way of describing the consideration of whether a task actually operationalises the intended psychological construct. A measure can be highly reliable, but this can stem from processes other than those which are believed or claimed to be captured by a particular task. At the extreme, measuring a person's height could be a highly *reliable* measure of attentional breadth, but likely a terrible one from the point of view of validity. In sections 2.7.3–2.7.6, I consider the issue of validity.

2.7.3 Distinguishing Process-Specific Variance from General Task Variance

Another potentially difficult issue when examining convergent and divergent associations is differentiating process-specific from general task variance. That is, performance on certain tasks can correlate because they have the same dependent variable (e.g., response time) due to generic factors such as the speed of an individual's motor responses or how they balance speed and accuracy demands (for a discussion of strategy in task performance, see Leber and Irons (2019)). These are separate from the underlying construct of interest (e.g., attentional breadth) (for an elaborated discussion, see Goodhew and Edwards (2019)). Any assessment of validity needs to separate out such generic factors from theoretical processes of interest.

This issue can be seen in the work of Onie and Most (2017). These authors examined the relationship between the effects of negatively emotionally salient stimuli that were not task relevant on attention and the extent to which this was associated with the experience of negative affect in everyday life. They assessed the variance in self-reported negative affect, as measured by the DASS (Lovibond & Lovibond, 1995). When operationalising attention, they employed paradigms that demonstrate the influence of emotion on attention, and crucially, selected one widely used measure of spatial attention in this domain: *the dot-probe* (Bar-Haim et al., 2007; Cox et al., 2017; MacLeod et al., 1986), and one important measure of temporal attention in this domain: *emotion-induced blindness* (Most, Chun, Widders, & Zald, 2005; Most, Smith, Cooter, Levy, & Zald, 2007). In the dot-probe, two images are presented simultaneously, typically for 500 ms, for example, one to the left and one to the right of fixation. One of these images is emotionally salient, and the other is not. These images disappear, and then a to-be-responded to probe appears in the location of one of the images. Participants' response efficiency to detect, identify, or localise the probe is gauged for when the probe appears behind the emotionally salient image versus the control image (side of presentation for an emotionally salient image is equally often left versus right). If participants are faster to identify the probe when it appears behind the emotionally salient stimulus, then it is said that attention was allocated to that image (Bar-Haim et al., 2007; Cox et al., 2017; MacLeod et al., 1986). Emotion-induced blindness stems from a rapid serial visual presentation of images is presented centrally. Participants' task is to identify the orientation of a landscape image that is rotated 90° to the left or right of vertical. Before this target, a distractor image is presented, which is either emotionally salient or emotionally neutral. The temporal lag between the distractor and target is varied. There is a deficit in target identification accuracy when the emotionally salient image appears close in time before the target. This occurs for both positive and negative relative to neutral images (Most et al., 2005; Most et al., 2007; Proud et al., 2020).

Onie and Most (2017) found that the dot-probe and emotion-induced blindness attentional interference effects from task-irrelevant negative versus neutral stimuli did not correlate with one another, and each was associated with unique variance in negative affect. The authors argued that attention is not a unitary concept, but instead that the distinction between spatial and temporal attention is important (Onie & Most, 2017). This is a laudable example of an evidence based dissociation between two laboratory tasks, more of this type of work needs to be carried out in relation to understanding how attentional breadth measures do or do not coalesce, and predict variance in meaningful outcome variables. Onie and Most (2017) attributed this divergence to the distinction between spatial and temporal attention, which is a possible candidate. The other key difference is that the dot-probe task is a response time-based measure (RT), whereas emotion-induced blindness is purely an accuracy based measure. It is possible that the reason that these tasks diverged relates to this difference, rather than a spatial/temporal distinction. RT and accuracy may not be related because it has been shown elsewhere that different types of attention can have divergent effects on them, such that only some aspects of attention affect accuracy (Prinzmetal, McCool, & Park, 2005). If accuracy and RT can have divergent effects, this candidate needs to be ruled out as an explanation for divergent effects across accuracy and RT measures. For example, it could be that the dot-probe and emotion-induced blindness actually reflect the same distracting effect of emotional salience on task performance, but failed to correlate just because of the different dependent variables employed. That said, it should be noted that accuracy and RT can correlate in some circumstances (Bruyer & Brysbaert, 2011).

It would be interesting to establish how an accuracy based dot-probe or a speed based emotion-induced blindness measure would fare. Would the spatial and temporal tasks still cleanly diverge? More broadly, this highlights the issue of distinguishing process-specific variance from task based variance in searching for convergence and divergence across measures of attentional breadth. For example, it will be important to establish that any convergence between the directed Navon and the flanker, is not only due to the common dependent variable of response time and that any divergence of the relationship between the flanker task and the breadth-of-attention task, is not only due to their different dependent variables. In factor analytic studies, the influence of generic task variance (e.g., RT) can be measured and controlled for explicitly, for example, Milne and Szczerbinski (2009).

This issue of task-general variance can also cloud estimates of reliability. It is often noted that difference scores (e.g., a global preference score obtained by subtracting RT in the local condition from RT in the global condition) have compromised reliability relative to raw scores (e.g., RT in the global condition). As discussed by Goodhew and Edwards (2019), however, this improved reliability for the raw score measures may be mediated via this task-general variance (e.g., the tendency for individuals to be relatively stable in their RTs across all conditions), rather than process-specific variance (e.g., the stability of attentional breadth measurement). This issue also needs to be considered in relation to quantifying the reliability of measurement.

Once measurement reliability is established, then measurement validity can be considered. In this section, the issue of the sources of variance was considered in relation to reliability and validity. In sections 2.7.3–2.7.6, I discuss some of the key criteria when assessing the validity of purported measures of attentional breadth. First, there should be convergent correlations between measures thought to reflect the same sub-process of attentional breadth, and weaker correlations with measures thought to reflect distinct processes. Second, measures of the same attentional breadth sub-process should show convergent effects of or on other variables, which diverge from measures of other sub-processes. Third, measures of attentional breadth should show convergent effects as revealed via neuroimaging. Each of these three criteria is discussed in more detail below (Sections 2.7.4-2.7.6).

2.7.4 Validity Assessment Via Correlations Among Attentional Breadth Measures

This criterion can be summarised as: if two measures do truly capture the variance of the same psychological process, then individuals' performance on the two tasks ought to correlate with one another. Moreover, this correlation ought to be higher than those observed between measures that do not gauge the same psychological process. Implementing this criterion requires consideration of all of the proceeding ones, including the hypothesised structure of attentional breadth, and the reliability of measurement, and the source of associations both within and between tasks.

At the broadest level, if we accept that there are (at least) two sub-processes of attentional breadth, then we would expect measures of each of these processes to show stronger relationships with one another (i.e., within process) than with measures of the other process (i.e., between process) if these are indeed distinct sub-processes of attentional breadth. By analogy, verbal and visuospatial intelligence are both forms of IQ and, therefore, will likely correlate with one another, but the correlation between different measures of verbal intelligence ought to be stronger than that between verbal and visuospatial measures if these are dissociable aspects of intelligence. Although there is little evidence for this conceptualisation, a common implicit assumption in the literature appears to be that attentional breadth is unitary. If so, then all measures of attentional breadth would need to demonstrate associations with each other in order to be deemed valid measures. Of course, such assessments of validity need to duly consider the reliability of measures, and the source of any consistent variance (i.e., is it process-specific). Furthermore, it is ideal for validity assessment if the same participants are tested on different measures at the same time, rather than drawing inferences about the strength of correlations between different samples tested at different times in different studies.

2.7.5 Attentional Breadth Measure Validity Assessment Via Associations With or Effects of Other Variables

As a criterion for validity, the effect of other variables should show similar effects on, or associations with, measures of the same purported process, and distinct effects on measures of different processes. When considering divergent evidence, the distinction between a single and double dissociation is a useful framework. A *single* dissociation is where variable A impacts process X but not process Y. This would be preliminary evidence that processes X and Y are distinct. However, there remain a number of more pedestrian explanations for this, such as that process X is more complex and, therefore, more susceptible to interference. A *double dissociation* is where variable A impacts process X and not process Y, *and* variable B impacts process Y but not process X. This is more definitive evidence that processes X and Y are truly distinct.

In the field of attentional breadth, a double dissociation between preference and control would be when a given experimental manipulation (e.g., manipulating cognitive load) affects performance on measures of control but not preference, in addition to a different experimental manipulation (e.g., mood) affecting performance on measures of preference but not control. This would be compelling evidence that preference and control are indeed distinct. The same double dissociation logic applies when considering relations with individual differences variables. That is, certain individual difference variables should doubly dissociate between the preference and control measures if they are truly independent aspects of attentional breadth.

Double dissociations are particularly powerful because they rule out more pedestrian explanations for observed single dissociations. For example, a participant's country of birth predicts their attentional breadth as measured by the undirected Navon task (McKone et al., 2010; see also the supplementary material of Goodhew & Plummer, 2019), such that participants born in an East Asian country (e.g., China) had a relatively greater advantage for global level versus local level targets compared with participants born in Australia. However, this group difference was not revealed when attentional breadth was gauged by the spatial distribution of IOR for Chinese versus Australian born participants (Lawrence, Edwards, Chan, Cox, & Goodhew, 2019). Is this because these two measures capture different sub-processes of attentional breadth? Or is it because the undirected Navon, at least the version employed in McKone et al., (2010), is simply more sensitive? Finding another variable for which the spatial distribution of IOR distinguishes among individual differences whereas the undirected Navon does not (i.e., moving from a single to a double dissociation) would refute a differential sensitivity explanation, thereby providing strong evidence for these gauging distinct processes or mechanisms. In addition, it should be noted that double dissociations are strongest when obtained in the same study on the same sample, to rule out sample-specific effects as an explanation for why dissociations occur as a function of a given variable (e.g., more pronounced group differences in the McKone et al., (2010) versus the Lawrence et al., (2019) study could also explain the effect on the Navon versus null effect on the spatial distribution of IOR).

2.7.6 Validity Assessment Via Neuroimaging

Neuroimaging can also provide useful insight regarding whether convergent patterns of neural activation occur following attention to different stimuli and tasks. We can never directly observe another person's covert attentional processes. However, one measure that arguably may get us closer than others is observing patterns of neural activation in different conditions which are claimed to operationalise attentional breadth. For example, attending to a global level of hierarchical stimuli on the one hand, and attending to a larger number of possible target locations on the other, both produce a zoom lens style pattern of activation in visual cortex (Müller, Bartelt, Donner, Villringer, & Brandt, 2003; Sasaki et al., 2001). That is, these studies found that the spatial extent of activation increased with increases in intended attentional breadth (e.g., as they went from attending to the local versus global elements) and that the magnitude of enhanced activation within this area diminished with increasing breadth. This evidence suggests that these two methods are convergent, such that they both reflect attentional breadth. Note that these authors were not specifically looking for this convergence in the design of their studies, but such convergences can be identified from a review of the literature. Further testing of the patterns of neural activation resulting from different measures of attentional breadth, with a deliberate view to looking for convergent and divergent evidence, should be useful in helping to identify and distinguish what aspect of attention or attentional breadth they truly capture.

It is important to bear in mind that neuroimaging may *not* be expected to necessarily reveal divergent effects of different sub-processes of attentional breadth. For example, attentional breadth control and preference may be distinct in how they are initiated. However, once initiated, the resulting attentional breadth may be equivalent in terms of its relationship with underlying neural activation. One individual could have a large attentional breadth because they prefer to, or because a task demanded them to, but either way, this may look like the same (broad) attentional breadth in terms of activation in primary visual cortex. This means that neuroimaging may not be ideal for distinguishing distinct sub-processes. (Alternatively, it may mean considering less visual-specific areas to isolate the different initiation mechanisms for control versus preference). Where it has excellent utility, is in the most basic question of all: does the measure under consideration actually operationalise attentional breadth at all?

2.8 Available Evidence on the Psychometrics and Structure of Attentional Breadth

In this section, I will discuss some of the possible processes that each of the introduced measures of attentional breadth capture, and evidence for the reliability and validity of these measures. At present, many measures of attentional breadth have not been assessed for their reliability or validity, but I will discuss what is available. The field currently lacks a clear theoretical model regarding the subcomponents of attentional breadth. However, we can take some clues from the existing evidence. As the analysis in this section will reveal, the overarching conclusion is that many of these attentional breadth tasks show divergent patterns and do not correlate with one another. A systematic study in which the interrelationships among a wide battery of attentional breadth measures including those described here has not yet been carried out and, therefore, here I will discuss where correlations and convergences among some of the measures have been reported.

While both the directed and undirected versions of the Navon task employ similar stimuli, it is thought that they operationalise distinct aspects of attentional breadth. The directed version of the Navon has been characterised as gauging participants' attentional breadth *control*, such as their ability to *set* a particular attentional breadth for a prolonged period of time. In contrast, the undirected version of the Navon (50/50% intermixed version) has been conceptualised as gauging participants' *preference* for adopting a global versus local attentional breadth, when the task requirements do not compel or favour (via either instruction or biased contingencies) adopting an attentional breadth that matches either the global or the local level (Caparos et al., 2013).

While the undirected Navon has been classified as a measure of attentional breadth preference, it is not clear precisely what participants are doing with their attention in this task. They could adopt their preferred attentional breadth (e.g., that which best matches the global level), and resize on any trial for which this does not match (e.g., any local trial). Alternatively, they could adopt an intermediate attentional breadth, and resize to either the global or local level from this intermediate. When these possibilities are considered, it is conceivable that the undirected version of the Navon actually gauges dynamic attentional *resizing*, rather than any static or default preference. This is not typically even noted when this task is used. This is striking since attentional resizing could be conceived of as a *control*-related function, potentially shifting the undirected Navon out of the category of preference measures. To summarise, more work is needed to understand all of the attentional processes underlying task performance with Navon stimuli.

How do responses to Kimchi and Palmer stimuli relate to the Navon? In one sense, they are essentially a variant of Navon stimuli. One of the most common stimuli used with Navon structures are letters, whereas for Kimchi and Palmer it is typically shapes. However, these are not defining differences, and different stimuli (e.g., letters and shapes,) can be used to create the global and local elements of either Navon or Kimchi and Palmer stimuli. Another common difference is that Kimchi and Palmer usually have relatively fewer local elements (e.g., just three or four), whereas Navon stimuli usually have more (although this appears to be a difference of degree, rather than kind, and also not a rigid demarcation). Most importantly, these stimuli are typically used in very different tasks. When participants are presented with Kimchi and Palmer stimuli, they are typically making a subjective judgement, one for which there is not an intrinsically correct or incorrect answer. That is, their choice reflects which they judge to look more similar, in a context in which both options have some similarities and some differences compared to the test stimulus. In this way, Kimchi and Palmer stimuli can be considered to provide a relatively pure gauge of attentional preference, where there are no task demands to find a prescribed target or speed requirements shaping their responses.

If Kimchi and Palmer measure attentional preference, while directed Navon measures the control of attentional breadth setting, then we should see divergences between directed Navon and Kimchi and Palmer measures. Existing evidence does suggest that the aspect of attentional breadth gauged in the standard Kimchi and Palmer task diverges from that measured in the directed version of the Navon task. The reason for this is twofold. First, Dale and Arnell (2013) have shown that these two measures of attentional breadth do not correlate with one another when both are measured reliably in the same group of participants. Second, they appear to diverge with respect to whether they are associated with stable traits, such as autism. Koldewyn et al. (2013) highlighted the distinction between ability (control) and preference in relation to attentional breadth and examined these in children with autism versus neurotypical controls. Those authors found that the group with autism showed an attentional breadth preference that was more locally inclined than their neurotypical counterparts, as measured with Kimchi and Palmer stimuli. When they used a directed Navon task, which required adopting an attentional breadth aligned with the global or local level (i.e., ability or control), and the magnitude of interference from the material at the task-irrelevant level was gauged, then both group of participants had similar levels of interference from the local and global competing levels. Although the autism group had larger interference scores overall relative to the neurotypical participants, this could be a product of the autism group having slower overall RTs (this is when a relative interference score could be more useful than an absolute difference score compared between groups, for an in-depth discussion see Goodhew, Dawel, and Edwards, (2020)). Crucially, interference effects were symmetric across global and local conditions for both groups. This divergence is consistent with the notion that directed Navon and Kimchi and Palmer tasks reflect dissociable aspects of attentional breadth, in particular: control over setting a particular attentional breadth for a relatively prolonged period when required by task demands versus preference, in the virtual absence of task demands respectively. Issues such as differential sensitivity to group differences across tasks could be more definitively ruled out via a double dissociation.

Moving on now to the UFOV and breadth-of-attention tasks, it would seem reasonable, given the nature of those tasks, to classify them as measures of *maximum* attentional breadth, under the umbrella of control-related functions. There is some evidence for this, but it is not overwhelming. Kreitz et al. (2015) found that individuals' performance on the breadth-of-attention task was correlated with their performance on the UFOV, which is a good start, and in stark contrast to the many divergences and absences of correlations between other measures of attentional breadth. However, the breadth-of-attention task was more strongly correlated with measures of working memory (2-back and AOSPAN) than it was to the UFOV. In fact, the correlation between the breadth-of-attention and working memory measures rivalled the strength of the relationship between the working memory measures themselves (Kreitz et al., 2015). This suggests that while they may be capturing some shared variance, there are clearly other cognitive processes that also contribute key variance to performance on the UFOV and breadth-of-attention tasks. This threatens the validity of these measures of attentional breadth. By analogy, if in the clinical literature a new measure of anxiety was proposed that correlated more strongly with existing measures of depression than anxiety, it would (justifiably) be difficult to justify this as a valid measure of anxiety.

The UFOV clearly captures meaningful variance that relates to important functional outcomes, such as driving performance, but whether the UFOV truly operationalises *attentional breadth* remains unclear. It has been suggested that impairments in UFOV performance are related to difficulties in disengaging attention, and unrelated to performance on other purported measures of attentional breadth, such as the flanker task (Cosman et al., 2012). It has also been found that training athletes on a variety of attentional tasks (including cueing, sustained attention, Stroop, and UFOV) leads to gains in performance on the breadth-of-attention task (Huttermann & Memmert, 2018). However, it is unknown whether it was the UFOV component in particular that was responsible for these improvements, or whether it was one or multiple of the other attentional tasks. Even if UFOV was a substantive contributor, there remains the issue of whether performance on the breadth-of-attention itself predominately reflects attentional breadth (Kreitz et al., 2015).

The variable of age has been found to show consistent associations with two different measures of attentional breadth, namely the spatial distribution of IOR when placeholders are absent (Lawrence et al., 2018), and the breadth-of-attention task (Huttermann et al., 2012). On both of these measures, age was associated with narrower attentional breadth. This converergence is interesting because the spatial distribution of IOR could be conceptualised as a measure of attentional preference, since there are few clear task demands to adopt a particular breadth, in contrast with the breadth-of-attention task in which a broader attentional breadth would be helpful and, therefore, is more likely a measure of attentional breadth control. However, perhaps the considerable spatial separation between the cue and target on some IOR trials does encourage a broadening of attention, like the breath-of-attention task, rendering them both measures of attentional breadth control. Taking a different perspective, it is possible that these are independent measures of preference and control and that older adults are both less likely and less able to adopt a broader attentional breadth. Alternatively, the consistent effect of age could reflect an intrinsic association between attentional breadth preference and control as they are both aspects of attentional breadth, even if they can be dissociated under other circumstances.

In a similar vein, working memory capacity has been found to predict participants' maximum attentional breadth as gauged by the breadth-of-attention task, such that higher capacity individuals had a larger maximum attentional breadth (Kreitz et al., 2015). Working memory has also been found to predict the ability to rapidly contract attention, as gauged using an adapted version of the flanker task (Heitz & Engle, 2007). This could be conceptualised as a metric of minimum attentional breadth. If so, then this is consistent with the notion that maximum and minimum attentional breadth may be related, because this other variable – working memory capacity – has convergent associations with both of them.

As previously stated, a participants' country of birth (e.g., Australia versus China), has been found to be associated with attentional breadth according to the undirected Navon (McKone et al., 2010), but not for the spatial distribution of IOR task (Lawrence et al., 2019). typically, these differences are attributed to ethnicity or culture, but terms like culture are not clearly defined, and not necessarily captured via the participants' country of birth, even though this is the measure most commonly used in cross-cultural research. These groups usually differ in other respects as well, which may be responsible for the observed group differences (e.g., domestic versus international students and the number of languages they are fluent in). However, even children (Canadian versus Japanese) differ in the way that they construct their drawings, which can be interpreted as reflecting a broad versus narrow attentional tendency and may rule out some (but definitely not all) of these competing explanations for the group differences (Senzaki, Masuda, & Nand, 2014). Putting aside the question of what psychological variable underlies the differences between individuals born in different countries. As discussed when the psychometric criteria were introduced, this single dissociation between the undirected Navon and the spatial distribution of IOR suggests that they may capture distinct processes, but stronger evidence would arise if a double dissociation were obtained and if this was found for the same group of participants to rule out sample-specific explanations (such as the potentially greater similarity between the two groups in the Lawrence et al. (2019) study).

In contrast with the many instances of apparent divergence, the effect of emotion (i.e., affect) is one that seems to be reasonably consistent across multiple measures of attentional breadth. For example, individuals who report high levels of anxiety and depression have been found to be more likely to choose the local over the global elements in the Kimchi and Palmer test (Basso et al., 1996), nominally a measure of attentional breadth preference. Similarly, experimentally induced negative mood states lead to a narrower attentional breadth preference, as gauged by the same type of Kimchi and Palmer test (Gasper & Clore, 2002), while positive mood states lead to a broader preference on the same measure (Fredrickson & Branigan, 2005). Even stimuli showing negative facial expressions have been found to reduce the flanker effect (Fenske & Eastwood, 2003), whereas experimentally induced positive moods and positive expression stimuli both increase flanker effects relative to neutral moods or stimuli (Fenske & Eastwood, 2003; Rowe et al., 2007). These patterns on the flanker task are consistent with the Kimchi and Palmer test results. This may indicate that this that these two measures reflect the same aspects of attentional breadth. However, it is also possible that emotion influences a host of distinct attentional, cognitive, and behavioural outcomes in consistent ways, without this necessitating that they all necessarily reflect the same underlying process. Indeed, the *motivational intensity* of emotion has been reported to affect memory as well as attention in convergent ways (Gable & Harmon-Jones, 2008, 2010b), but this does not necessarily mean that memory and attention are the same cognitive process. In this way, double dissociations are more compelling evidence of a distinction than convergence is of a unitary underlying construct.

To my knowledge, the published literature does not provide measures of association between many of the above measures, which would be useful in piecing together an underlying architecture and assessing the validity of individual measures. This means that we do not know, for example, whether flanker interference for a spatially fixed target correlates with flanker interference for a spatially variant target, whether either flanker measure correlates with performance on the breadth-of-attention task, or whether the spatial gradient of IOR correlates with response to the Kimchi and Palmer stimuli. There is clearly more work to be done in this space.

2.9 Measuring Attentional Breadth: Future Directions in Conceptualisation

When authors refer to attentional breadth or concepts that are considered related if not synonymous with it, the implicit assumption invoked is that there is some broader latent variable that meaningfully encapsulates these different processes and measures. However, we are yet to see clear evidence for such a construct, and even if there is one, attentional breadth is unlikely to be a monolithic construct and, indeed, there is scant evidence for such a conceptualisation. Instead, there seems to be value in the distinction between measures of preference versus control. Notably, this is reminiscent of other distinctions in the existing literature on other aspects of attention, which also distinguish attentional control from other processes (Corbetta & Shulman, 2002, 2011). In the context of breadth, attentional breadth preference refers to differences both between and within individuals in the breadth-of-attention they adopt in the face of a given stimulus or scene, either in the absence of task requirements, or when the task requirements to not compel adopting a particular attentional breadth. Here, some individuals tend to go broader while others go narrower, and state variables such as emotion can also influence this tendency. (Note that with respect to the term 'preference' I refer to an attentional tendency, and am agnostic about whether this is accompanied by an explicit awareness of this tendency, or an emotional response to adopting that breadth). In contrast, control refers to how well one can resize to and sustain a given attentional breadth. In the extremes, there is the minimum and maximum attentional breadth one is capable of instantiating, and another important control-related process is how effectively and efficiently one is able to dynamically change the size of their attentional breadth. It remains unclear whether these are related to measures of preference (e.g., is one's maximum attentional breadth larger if one has a larger attentional preference?) or whether these are independent. Even within control-based measures, it is possible that tasks are tapping different processes or parts of the process. In a nutshell, it will be important for future research to state more clearly precisely which aspect or aspects of attentional breadth they are *aiming* to study. That is, at present, there is fuzziness in the theoretical development of attentional breadth, and this stems in no small part from a series of very different tasks all being classified under a singular umbrella when further differentiation is needed. Once there is greater clarity on the theoretical side of things, another major challenge that we face as a field is whether these tasks actually measure the psychological construct that we intend it to.

2.10 Measuring Attentional Breadth: Conclusion

In conclusion, there are many different measures of attentional breadth. Attentional breadth is unlikely to be a unitary concept, and the limited associations between different measures may reflect a multifaceted concept of attentional breadth. At present, there is a lack of clarity in the literature about what the important subcomponents are. Developing and testing models (e.g., proposing that attentional breadth preference and control are independent) will likely prove a productive avenue forward for future research. A greater focus on the validity of tasks as the operationalisations of these processes is also required. I have identified several types of evidence that will be useful in validity testing measures and latent structures of attentional breadth. This will require tackling some measurement issues such as reliability, and differentiating process-specific from general variance. If these issues are addressed, then essentially a factor analysis on a large swathe of measures of attentional breadth could prove to be a very useful contribution to the field. This will provide insight into how variance from the different measures coalesce (or not) onto different underlying factors.

3 Manipulating Attentional Breadth and Understanding Its Impact on Performance

The focus of this section is on the visual task performance consequences of having a particular sized attentional breadth at a given point in time. That is when participants have a broad versus narrow attentional breadth, what impact does this have on perceptual or other attentional processes? Typically, this is tested by inducing and maintaining a set attentional breadth either for the course of a single experimental trial, or more commonly for a series of trials (e.g., an experimental block), and then measuring the impact of this on another process via another task. These outcome visual tasks include those that gauge perceptual, attentional, and cognitive processes. Note that this is different from section 2, which focussed on *measures* of attentional breadth. Now, attentional breadth is the independent variable (i.e., manipulated to be broad versus narrow), and performance on the outcome visual task is the dependent variable.

This section will encompass both a discussion of common methods that have been used to manipulate attentional breadth (i.e., a descriptive approach), and provide recommendations regarding some key criteria that approaches to manipulating attentional breadth and investigating its impact on visual task performance need to satisfy in order for sound conclusions to be drawn (i.e., a prescriptive approach). In doing so, I will highlight how existing examples in the literature have fallen prey to methodological issues that could distort the conclusions that are drawn from them. Then, I will provide an overview of the theoretical developments in this area, starting with the historic and now classic zoom-lens model, and then moving onto models that have since been proposed, and describe and discuss the evidence for and against these models. This theoretical discussion will also refer back to methodological issues, which have had a key influence on model testing. Finally, I will discuss future directions for model development in relation to understanding the impact of attentional breadth on visual perception and performance.

3.1 Manipulating Attentional Breadth to Study Its Impact on Perception: Approaches in the Literature

Manipulating attentional breadth and then measuring its impact on visual perception and performance typically entails presenting a stimulus designed to manipulate the breadth of attention, and then presenting another stimulus designed to measure the resulting impact on visual perception. Typically, this entails different methods from those used to measure attentional breadth (with exceptions, such as directed Navon, interference scores provide a measure of attentional breadth control, but directing participants to attend to the global versus local level can also serve as an experimental manipulation of attentional breadth). Often shapes or stimuli of different sizes are used to manipulate attentional breadth. That is, a small shape is designed to induce a narrow attentional breadth, whereas a large shape is designed to induce a broad attentional breadth. In some designs, these shapes are merely presented on some or all of the trials (Benso, Turatto, & Gastone, 1998; Castiello & Umiltà, 1990; Mounts & Edwards, 2017), in others, participants are required to make a response about the shape to ensure that they are engaged with and attending to it (Goodhew & Edwards, 2016; Goodhew, Lawrence, & Edwards, 2017; Goodhew et al., 2016). For example, the shape-inducer method entails presenting small (to manipulate narrow attentional breadth) or large (to manipulate broad attentional breadths) shapes on 80 per cent of trials in a block. The shapes are either circles, or subtly deformed circles into ellipses, and participants' task on these trials is to indicate whether a circle or ellipse was presented. On the remaining 20 per cent of trials (randomly intermixed), participants are presented with a stimulus designed to measure their perceptual acuity. For example, a small circle that has a gap on either its left or right. Here, spatial acuity for the identical stimuli is enhanced in the small-shape block condition relative to the large-shape block condition (Goodhew et al., 2017; Goodhew et al., 2016).

Directed Navon tasks have also been used to manipulate attentional breadth, whereby attending to the global stimuli is designed to induce a broad attentional breadth whereas attending to the local stimuli has been intended to induce a narrow attentional breadth (Gable & Harmon-Jones, 2011; Gao et al., 2011; Macrae & Lewis, 2002). Changing the perceptual or cognitive load of an array is also believed to alter attentional breadth (Lavie, 2005), which can be used as a manipulation from which the performance consequences are studied (Ahmed & de Fockert, 2012). For example, the perceptual load can be increased by increasing the number of non-target items that are similar to the target, and this is thought to narrow the breadth-of-attention. Cognitive load can be increased by the addition of a working memory task, which is thought to broaden attentional breadth (Ahmed & de Fockert, 2012; Lavie, 2005).

Visual search efficiency has also been used to manipulate the breadth-of-attention. The logic here is a highly efficient visual search broadens the scope of attention while an inefficient one narrows it, and this manipulation has been found to influence performance on other visual tasks interspersed between the visual search task (Chong & Treisman, 2005). In addition, placing an outline shape of a given size over a visual search array is claimed to manipulate attentional breadth, such that a smaller shape results in a narrower attentional breadth (Greenwood & Parasuraman, 1999, 2004). This represents a sample of some of the main ways to manipulate attentional breadth but is not an exhaustive list. In section 3.2, I will describe some of the pitfalls that these different methods can fall prey to and offer a number of criteria which designs ought to satisfy in order to validly operationalise attentional breadths of different sizes and meaningfully measure the corresponding perceptual and performance consequences. First, some of these outcomes will be described.

Methods which claim to manipulate attentional breadth have led to outcomes such as enhanced response efficiency for target detection (Benso et al., 1998; Castiello & Umiltà, 1990), superior spatial acuity (Balz & Hock, 1997; Goodhew & Edwards, 2016; Goodhew et al., 2016), and improved perception of high spatial frequencies (Goodhew et al., 2017) under a narrow relative to a broad attentional breadth. In contrast, the psychological processes that have been suggested to benefit from a broader attentional breadth include face and object perception (Gao et al., 2011; Gerlach & Starrfelt, 2018; Macrae & Lewis, 2002), visual search (Belopolsky, Zwaan, Theeuwes, & Kramer, 2007;

Greenwood & Parasuraman, 1999, 2004), the processing of summary scene statistics (Chong & Treisman, 2005), change detection (Pringle, Irwin, Kramer, & Atchley, 2001), the perception of happy facial expressions (Srinivasan & Hanif, 2010), and the prioritisation of threat-related information (Notebaert, Crombez, Van Damme, Durnez, & Theeuwes, 2013). Even complex functional outcomes such as driving performance have been linked to broadened attentional breadth (Ball et al., 1993). Some perceptual processes, such as temporal acuity (as measured by tasks such as temporal gap detection), have been the subject of mixed findings and debate (Goodhew et al., 2016; Lawrence, Edwards, & Goodhew, 2020; Mounts & Edwards, 2017; for a review see Lawrence, Edwards, Talipski, & Goodhew, 2020). Finally, attentional breadth influences the perception of ambiguous stimuli, such that a broadened breadth has been found to increase reports of group (versus element) motion in the Ternus display (Hock, Park, & Schoner, 2002). In contrast, some processes, such as object individuation (as measured by the object substitution masking paradigm), appear invariant to attentional breadth manipulations (Goodhew, 2017; Goodhew & Edwards, 2016).

3.2 Manipulating Attentional Breadth: Important Principles

Here five important design principles are considered in relation to manipulating attentional breadth. In doing so, I provide examples of studies from the literature which have violated these principles and discuss the implications that this has for their interpretation. The goal here is *not* to chastise any individual researcher (indeed I critically analyse a paradigm that I was instrumental in introducing). Instead, it is to highlight and discuss these issues so that all researchers can learn from them so that all future research can be immune to them.

3.2.1 Compare Conditions Which Both Entail an Attended Target

When comparing how visual perception or performance fares for different attentional breadths, it is important that in both conditions (e.g., the narrow focus of attention and broad focus of attention conditions), the stimuli which serve as measures of visual perception are both attended. Otherwise, the comparison is between the presence versus absence of attention, rather than narrow versus broad attentional breadth (see Figure 7).

Consider the study by Notebaert et al. (2013), where the authors examined the influence of the size of the attentional window (i.e., attentional breadth) on the prioritisation of threatening information. Their conclusion was that a broader attentional window leads to enhanced prioritisation of threat. However, the

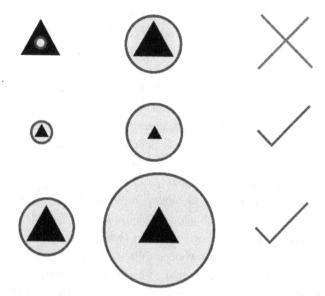

Figure 7 An illustration of the issue of having attentional breadths that exclude the stimuli used to gauge the effect of attentional breadth on performance. The black triangles are the stimuli used to gauge the impact of attentional breadth on perception, and ellipses with outlines indicate hypothetical attentional breadths. The perceptual stimuli should always appear within the attentional breadth in all conditions, and all that ought to change is the size of this region.

results could equally be recast as showing that threatening information is prioritised when it is attended, compared with when it is not.

In an attempt to manipulate attentional breadth, Notebaert et al. (2013), adapted a paradigm first introduced by Belopolsky et al. (2007). That is, Notebaert et al. (2013) employed a go/no-go task, where whether participants ought to respond or withhold their response was indicated to them via either a small or a large aspect of the display. Specifically, they were instructed that their response was determined by either the shape of the fixation stimulus (designed to narrow attentional breadth) or the shape of the whole configuration of the stimuli in the array (designed to broaden attentional breadth). To manipulate *threat*, they classically conditioned participants to the stimulus of a particular colour. That is, for each participant one colour was associated with an 'electrocutenaous stimulus' (i.e., an electric shock), which participants learned during an acquisition phase. Following this, to gauge attentional prioritisation, participants performed a visual search task on the stimuli in the array, which consisted of discs with a circumference of colour and a line inside each. The target was defined as a particular orientation (e.g., vertical) line inside the disc. Set size (i.e., the number of items in the search array) varied from three to six. To gauge whether threat-related information was prioritised, search times to find the target were considered as a function of when the target appeared inside a disc surrounded by the threat-related colour (congruent trials), compared with when a non-target appeared inside the shock associated colour (incongruent trials). It was found that this congruency manipulation did not impact search times for the local condition, whereas it did for the global condition (Notebaert et al., 2013). More specifically, in the global condition, search times increased less steeply from a set size of three to six when the target appeared inside the threat relevant colour than it did for when a non-target appeared inside the threat relevant colour. This relative search advantage did not occur in the local condition and, instead, all conditions showed a proportionate increase in response time as set size increased. This led to the conclusion that a broadened attentional breadth enhances attentional prioritisation of threat-related information (Notebaert et al., 2013).

If we assume that in the condition where attention was allocated to the fixation dot, the size of the attentional breadth was roughly equivalent to the size of the fixation dot, then in this condition no stimuli other than the fixation dot appeared within this region. Therefore, the threat-related information was likely to be always *outside* of the attended region. This means that the findings from this paradigm probably show that threat-related information is prioritised when it is *attended*, versus when it was *not attended*. Of course, this critique assumes that participants do not adjust their attentional breadth after identifying the fixation stimulus. I cannot rule out the possibility that participants expanded their attention to a breadth larger than the fixation. However, if this occurred, then this paradigm may tell us more about the dynamics of attentional resizing, rather than inform us clearly about the effect of a given attentional breadth per se. Ultimately, we are left with uncertainty about the attentional processes that were occurring in this design. If we truly want to be able to conclude that the size of one's attentional breadth affects whether threat-related information is prioritised, then we need to compare two blocks of trials, where the threat-related information is attended to in both, and all that changes is the size of the attentional breadth in that block. That is, to compare a relatively *narrow* attentional breadth which consistently encompasses the critical stimulus with a relatively *broad* attentional breadth which also consistently encompasses the critical stimulus.

3.2.2 Compare Performance for Stimuli at the Same Eccentricity

Perceptual acuity (especially spatial acuity) declines dramatically with increasing eccentricity. Therefore, it is not a fair comparison of different attentional breadths to have the test stimuli for assessing performance outcomes appear at different eccentricities to one another (for a similar argument, see Lawrence, Edwards, Talipski, et al. (2020)).

An example of a study that fell victim to this issue was one that was carried out by Kosslyn et al. (1999), who concluded that older adults have difficulty focussing their attention on a larger region of space (i.e., have difficulty adopting a broader attentional breadth). This conclusion was based on methods whereby the to-be-responded-to stimulus array either expanded into the periphery or contracted toward fixation. The stimuli were four boxes arranged in a plus-sign shape around fixation, and Xs appeared in one or two of these boxes. The participants' task was to indicate whether there were Xs in one or two of the boxes. These authors found that older adults were disproportionally slower to make this response when the stimuli expanded into the periphery. There are known changes in basic sensory processes associated with ageing (Owsley, 2011). Therefore, whenever studying the effects of ageing on attention, it is important to design it in a way that these sensory effects cannot account for any impairment observed. This was not done by Kosslyn et al. (1999), so it is unclear whether older adults do indeed have difficulty adopting a broader attentional breadth, or whether the results were a demonstration of the known decrement in sensory acuity for more peripherally presented stimuli that may have disproportionately affected older adults[4]. This issue is not limited to ageing. Any outcome-measure performance comparison between different levels of another variable (including attentional breadth: small versus large) should not conflate differences in the eccentricity of the stimuli. Note that it may be necessary to have inducers that are centred on the same point but extend into different eccentricities – it is outcome measures that need to be eccentricity-matched. This highlights the principle that it is important to compare visual task performance for stimuli at the same eccentricity. So that changes in attentional breadth are not conflated with *shifts* of attention, it is ideal to measure performance for centrally presented (foveal, fixated) stimuli.

3.2.3 Ensure That Attentional Breadth, Rather Than Shifts of Attention, Are What is Being Manipulated.

Changes in the scale of attentional breadth are conceptually distinct from changes in the central focus of attention (e.g., attentional shifts or orienting)

---

[4] It should be noted that peripheral stimuli were also used in Lawrence et al. (2018), however, crucially, this study found that it was selective when placeholders were absent that older adults demonstrated a narrower attentional breadth, not when placeholders were present. This selectivity rules out an eccentricity based explanation of the results, and instead points to an attentional one.

and, therefore, should be operationalised independently. When the goal is to understand the performance consequences of the breadth of the putative spotlight of attention, such effects should not be contaminated with shifts in the central location of this spotlight. Shifts of attention are known to have their own measurable perceptual consequences in isolation (Yeshurun & Carrasco, 1998; Yeshurun & Levy, 2003) and, therefore, if both a shift and rescale of attention occur, any observed perceptual consequences could be a product of either the shift or rescale, or a synergistic combination of them (this synergy, of course, could be a research question once the perceptual consequences of each in isolation are understood. However, until we have a firmer understanding of the effects of attentional breadth on perception, it is preferable if they are studied separately). In a similar vein, it is important that any manipulation of broad attention compels the spreading of a contiguous attended region of attention over a large area, rather than multiple shifts of a narrow breadth-of-attention over a large area.

An example of a probable failure to do this is from Fang et al. (2017). These authors sought to address the interesting question of whether attentional breadth could be trained on one task, and would transfer to another. However, it is apparent that one of their tasks likely reflected the rapid shifting of a narrow spotlight of attention, rather than a true change in breadth. To manipulate a broad attentional breadth, participants were presented with an array of multiple letters (e.g., multiple Ts and Hs), and under one condition, their task was to report the identity of the letter furthest from fixation. Evidence from elsewhere indicates that when the target is not easily differentiated from distractors in its features like this, then it is likely to induce a narrow focus of attention, especially given the presence of similar and spatially close distractors which need to be filtered out (Chong & Treisman, 2005; Goodhew & Clarke, 2016). This narrow attentional breadth will be moved around from one location to another (i.e., a series of shifts of attention) to perform the visual search. Therefore, it is unlikely that this task did, in fact, manipulate a broad attentional breadth. This means that the study cannot be used to draw any definite conclusions about the trainability of attentional breadth. The take-home message is that it is important to ensure that any paradigms used to manipulate attentional breadth are not more likely to induce a different attentional process, such as shifts of attention.

As discussed in Section 2 where the breadth-of-attention task was introduced (Huttermann et al., 2012; Huttermann & Memmert, 2015; Huttermann et al., 2014), when two configurations of shapes are presented on opposing sides of a screen, it is possible that participants either split their attention between these two locations (i.e., have two distinct attention regions, one at each stimulus location) or rapidly shift a single (small) attentional breadth from one to the other. While to date the breadth-of-attention task has been used as a measure, rather than manipulation of attentional breadth, it is important to highlight this issue, so that the potential for splits or shifts is minimised in future experiments aiming to manipulate attentional breadth. The most viable solutions overlap with those for preventing annuli of attention are as per those discussed in section 3.2.4, that is, having inducing stimuli that are continuous over the desired attended region.

3.2.4 Ensure That Attentional Breadth Is Manipulated, Rather Than an Annulus of Attention or Multiple Split Regions Being Created

Attention can be reshaped into an annulus (i.e., a doughnut shape) under certain circumstances (Jefferies & Di Lollo, 2015). Specifically, while previous literature on whether attention can be deployed in the form of an annulus was somewhat mixed, Jefferies and Di Lollo (2015) obtained compelling evidence that attention can take an annulus shape *if the right spatial structure is present to facilitate this*. These authors used a paradigm in which multiple rapid serial visual presentation (RSVP) streams appeared in four peripheral locations containing task-relevant stimuli, in addition to a stream of distractors appearing in the centre of the screen. If attention can be deployed in the form of an annulus, then participants should be able to attend to the peripheral locations while not attending to the centre stream. Jefferies and Di Lollo (2015) varied whether placeholders were present at the four locations of the streams or not, thereby manipulating the presence/absence of spatial structure which could facilitate an annulus of attention. It was found that participants were not affected by the centre stream when the placeholders were present, whereas they were affected by the centre stream when the placeholders were absent. This same result held even when eight peripheral locations were used. The inference from this pattern of results is that in the presence of the placeholders, participants were able to adopt an attentional annulus that excluded the centre region from the focus of attention, whereas they could do not this when placeholders were absent (Jefferies & Di Lollo, 2015). Elsewhere it has been suggested that individuals with high working memory capacity may be particularly able to create annuli of attention (Bleckley et al., 2003).

Such reshaping processes are dissociable from that of controlling the setting of a particular attentional breadth. However, some popular methods for manipulating attentional breadth may have inadvertently been shaping an annulus of attention (with a hole in the middle), rather than a creating a continuous (approximately elliptical) zone of attention spread over a wide area. This is because it is common in the literature to use unfilled or outline shapes to induce different attentional breadths. For example, a large outline circle would be intended to induce a broader attentional breadth, while a small outline circle would be intended to induce a narrower attentional breadth (Benso et al., 1998; Castiello & Umiltà, 1990; Goodhew et al., 2016; Greenwood & Parasuraman, 2004; Yeshurun & Carrasco, 2008). This is potentially problematic because this is precisely the kind of spatial structure that encourages attention to adopt an annulus shape (Jefferies & Di Lollo, 2015). Recent work has shown that a qualitatively different pattern of results on spatial and temporal acuity is obtained when an outline shape is used to manipulate attentional breadth (Goodhew et al., 2016) compared with when a global motion stimulus is used as an attentional breadth inducer, which compels the spreading of attention across the entire region (Lawrence, Edwards, & Goodhew, 2020). That is, both psychophysical and electrophysiological evidence indicates that perceiving global motion in such stimuli compels the pooling of information across the entire region (Burr, Concetta Morrone, & Vaina, 1998; Tanaka & Saito, 1989). This implicates distinct attentional processes in the two different studies, which is likely attributable to an annulus of attention when outline shapes are used, versus a true change in attentional breadth when a global motion inducer is used.

There is currently no direct evidence that an annulus of attention was created via the shape-inducer task. However, given the prior evidence that this kind of spatial structure was the type that facilitates an annulus of attention, and the evidence that global motion stimuli do compel the pooling of information across the entire stimulus region, in conjunction with the qualitatively different pattern of results stemming from the different types of inducers, strongly suggest that this is a likely possibility. Therefore, outline shapes should be avoided as stimuli for manipulating different attentional breadths (see also Lawrence, Edwards, Talipski, et al. (2020)). Instead, stimuli which encourage the spread of attention across the entire region should be used, such as global motion or Glass pattern stimuli of different sizes (Lawrence, Edwards, & Goodhew, 2020), identifying the local versus global elements of Navon stimuli (Gable & Harmon-Jones, 2011; Hanif et al., 2012), and performing efficient versus inefficient visual search (Chong & Treisman, 2005) (see Figure 8). The global motion/Glass pattern inducers also have the clear advantage of directly being able to specify the size of each attentional breadth, thereby avoiding some of the methodological issues identified earlier (e.g., having the narrow attentional breadth exclude part of the target stimulus).

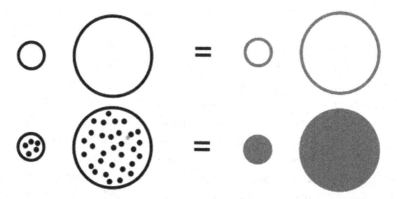

Figure 8 An illustration of what different inducers (left hand side) are believed to do to attentional breadth (right hand side). Outline shapes likely create an annulus of attention where attention is absent inside the shape, whereas inducers that compel participants to pool across the entire region (e.g., global motion task on moving dots) encourage attention to spread over the entire stimulus region and, therefore, are a more appropriate technique for manipulating attentional breadth.

3.2.5 Ensure That Attentional Breadth is the Source of Any Benefit, Not Just a Cue Which Facilitates the Process Under Study Via Unrelated Means

It has been claimed that the visual search for a letter target is facilitated by a narrow breadth of attention, in both feature and conjunction searches (Greenwood & Parasuraman, 1999, 2004). However, this conclusion arose from a study in which the manipulation of attentional breadth simply involved placing the outline of a box over part of the visual search array, and the target always appeared inside this box. The size of this box was varied to manipulate different sizes of attentional breadth. It was found that the smaller the size of this box, the faster visual search times became. It is possible that participants narrowed the focus of their attention to correspond to the size of the outline box. But it is also possible that the breadth of their attention was unchanged and, instead, the box simply demarcated the area over which they had to search. This box may have reduced the number of items needing to be searched, and impacted search times because of this reason, unrelated to attentional breadth. A similar outcome could have been produced via verbal instruction such as 'the target is one of the four stimuli in the top left hand corner'. Of course, such cues may still instigate attentional processes, but could produce benefits in visual search efficiency without changing the size of the attended region per se. Therefore, it is important to ensure that it is *attentional breadth*, rather than other attentional or cognitive processes, that is the source of any observed benefit.

3.3 Theory Development Regarding the Visual Task Performance Consequences of Attentional Breadth

This section entails changing gears from a methodology and operationalisation focus, to a theoretical one.

3.3.1 Zoom-Lens Model

The 1980s marked some seminal contributions to the measurement of human attention. For example, Posner developed the cueing paradigm, which offered a method for gauging where in space one's focus of attention is located, and the process of shifting that locus through space (Posner, 1980; Posner et al., 1980). This paradigm assumes a relatively small, fixed width singular focus of attention. Eriksen and St. James (1986) were critical of the notion that the focus of spatial attention has a fixed width. Instead, they proposed the *Zoom-Lens Model,* according to which people can change the scale of their visual attention across space. Moreover, this model espouses a tradeoff between the size of the attended area and the magnitude of perceptual enhancement. That is, when attention is focussed on a relatively narrow space, then the magnitude of perceptual enhancement for stimuli within that region is greater than when attention is spread diffusely over a larger area, where the magnitude of enhancement for any given location within the attended region is relatively weaker. Eriksen and St. James (1986) obtained evidence consistent with the zoom-lens model. To test this, the authors used displays in which they presented eight letters in an imaginary circle, and underlined particular ones to cue different numbers of them (and, therefore, change the size of the participant's attentional breadth). Participants' task was to identify which of two possible letter targets appeared. There was evidence for this tradeoff, such that response time increased with the size of the cued display. For example, response time increased when one versus four stimuli were cued, whereas there was no difference between four versus eight. This is consistent with the idea that attentional breadth conformed to a roughly circular shape, such that when four items were cued attention encompassed the entire circular array, and therefore there was no increased cost for additionally cued items. In contrast, when only one item was cued, attention could be more focussed on that single item and had to expand to accommodate an increase in the number of cued items (Eriksen & St. James, 1986).

In addition to demonstrating that attentional breadth can be modified, the zoom- lens model prescribes a specific relationship between the size of the attended region and the corresponding visual task performance outcomes. That is, that a smaller attentional breadth leads to larger magnitude performance enhancement relative to a larger attentional breadth. There is both behavioural and more recent neuroimaging evidence to support this model. Namely, response efficiency increases the smaller the attentional breadth, which has been shown via both the original method to induce attentional breadth and more modern incarnations of it (Eriksen & St. James, 1986; Müller et al., 2003). Spatial acuity has been found to be enhanced for a narrower attentional breadth via a variety of attentional breadth induction methods (Balz & Hock, 1997; Goodhew et al., 2016; Lawrence, Edwards, & Goodhew, 2020). Activation in the primary visual cortex also shows this tradeoff between the area of enhance-ment and the magnitude of perceptual enhancement within that area when the size of the attended region is changed (Müller et al., 2003).

In their proposal of the zoom-lens model, Eriksen, and St. James (1986) did not specify which specific aspects of perception of this applies to. Because no differentiation was made, it is reasonable to infer that the model assumes that this relationship holds for all aspects of visual perception. Alternatively, if one does not agree with this inference, then the zoom-lens model is silent about which aspects of perception conform to this model and, therefore, further testing and development of the model are required. This means that irrespective of which interpretation one favours, the avenue forward is consistent, namely, testing whether or not the effects of attentional breadth are uniform across different aspects of perception.

3.3.2 Pathway-Specific Models of the Outcomes of Attentional Breadth

One of the most major demarcations in the human brain is the one between the *dorsal* and *ventral* cortical streams. That is, the dorsal stream can be thought of as the 'where' (or 'how') pathway, in that it preferentially processes stimulus properties such as motion, and is implicated in visually guided reaching. In contrast, the ventral stream can be conceptualised as the 'what' pathway, in that it preferentially processes stimulus information such as form and identity and underlies processes such as object recognition (Goodale & Milner, 1992; Mishkin, Ungerleider, & Macko, 1983). While there is considerable overlap in the processing priorities of these two streams, and they interact extensively, there is an underlying specialisation of function that differentiates them. It is possible that particular attentional breadths have a consistent impact on all different aspects of visual perception (including those mediated predominately by the two different pathways), as can be inferred from the zoom-lens model. However, several models have proposed that attentional breadth has differential effects on perceptual processes that are predominately mediated by one versus the other of these pathways[5]. This section will discuss these models. First, I will discuss this major pathway distinction in more detail.

The dorsal and ventral cortical streams have differential relationships with the magnocellular and parvocellular pathways, which connect the retina to the cortex via the lateral geniculate nucleus (LGN). These relationships are ones of differences in the degree of connection, not kind (i.e., predominate rather than exclusive relationships). The dorsal cortical stream is predominately innervated by the magnocellular pathway, whereas the ventral stream receives more balanced input from both the magnocellular and the parvocellular pathways (Ferrera, Nealey, & Maunsell, 1992). The magnocellular pathway is specialised for processing rapid changes in luminance across *time* (i.e., high temporal frequencies), such as abrupt object appearances and disappearances, and motion. In contrast, the parvocellular pathway is specialised for processing rapid changes in luminance across space (i.e., high spatial frequencies), such as that which underlies the high fidelity processing of fine spatial detail (Denison, Vu, Yacoub, Feinberg, & Silver, 2014; Derrington & Lennie, 1984; Livingstone & Hubel, 1988; Schiller & Logothetis, 1990; Schiller, Logothetis, & Charles, 1990). In real-world vision, all visual processing involves both the magnocellular and parvocellular pathways and the dorsal and ventral cortical streams. However, different perceptual processes will call upon them differentially. For example, perceiving high speed motion would recruit greater magnocellular and dorsal involvement, whereas perceiving detailed form information would recruit greater parvocellular and ventral involvement.

Given that this dorsal/ventral (and related magnocellular/parvocellular) demarcation is such an important distinction in the human brain, it is reasonable to consider the possibility that attention may differentially affect perceptual processes that are specialised for one stream versus the other. It is of note that most of the early testing of the effects of attentional breadth on visual perception entailed identifying small letters (Eriksen & St. James, 1986; LaBerge, 1983), that is, visual stimuli that demand relatively high spatial acuity and, therefore, would likely preferentially recruit the parvocellular pathway. From this, it is

---

[5] Note that here it will be assumed that attention directly impacts the visual signals that the human brain processes. *Visual perception* is an outcome from the processing operations that occur on these signals (both within and between streams).

unclear whether similar effects of attentional breadth occur for more magno-cellular-mediated aspects, such as temporal acuity.

Support for this idea that the perceptual consequences of attentional breadth may be pathway-specific also arises from the finding that transient *shifts* of attention have been found to have differential effects on spatial versus temporal resolution, consistent with a tradeoff in the relative contribution of the parvo-cellular versus magnocellular pathways to visual perception (Yeshurun & Levy, 2003; Yeshurun & Marom, 2008; Yeshurun & Sabo, 2012). In particular, transient attentional shifts have been found to impair temporal resolution, but enhance spatial resolution, indicative of a bias toward parvocellular processing and against magnocellular processing. Indeed, this notion of magnocellular/parvocellular perceptual tradeoff has proliferated in cognate literature, such as the perceptual consequences of emotion (Bocanegra & Zeelenberg, 2011), and of hand proximity to visual stimuli (Goodhew, Edwards, Ferber, & Pratt, 2015; Gozli, West, & Pratt, 2012; Thomas, 2015).

Two visual pathway-specific models of the impact of attentional breadth on perception have been proposed. The first was the Spatiotemporal Trade-off model (Bush & Vecera, 2014; Goodhew et al., 2016; for an earlier forerunner of these ideas, see Shulman, Sullivan, Gish, & Sakoda, 1986), which advocated that a narrower attentional breadth would lead to enhanced parvocellular-mediated visual processes (e.g., spatial acuity), whereas a broader attentional breadth would lead to enhanced magnocellular-mediated visual processes (e.g., temporal acuity). These predictions are derived from the fact that parvocellular neurons have relatively smaller receptive fields relative to magnocellular neurons, in addition to having differential spatial and temporal selectivity (Denison et al., 2014; Derrington & Lennie, 1984; Livingstone & Hubel, 1988; Schiller et al., 1990). Therefore, the idea is that magnocellular neurons may be preferentially recruited in the instantiation of a broader attentional breadth, and parvocellular neurons in narrower attentional breadths, resulting in a qualitative change in spatial versus temporal acuity across changes in the size of attentional breadth. Explicit testing of the Spatiotemporal Trade-off model (using the shape-inducer method) failed to find support for it (Goodhew et al., 2016). Instead, it was found that when participants were attending to smaller outline shapes for a block of trials, their spatial acuity was enhanced relative to when they were attending to larger outline shapes. However, there was no impact of this manipulation on temporal acuity (Goodhew et al., 2017; Goodhew et al., 2016; but see Mounts & Edwards, 2017).

This finding that spatial acuity but not temporal acuity was enhanced failed to support the Spatiotemporal Temporal Trade-off model and led to the proposal of the Selective Spatial Enhancement (SSE) model. Since predominately parvocellular-mediated visual processing (e.g., spatial acuity) dramatically declines in resolution with increasing eccentricity, the SSE model proposes that the consequences of attentional breadth are specific to enhancing parvocellular-mediated perceptual processes under a narrow attentional breadth (Goodhew et al., 2017; Goodhew et al., 2016). (For a similar idea about covert shifts of attention, see Carrasco (2011)). Consistent with this, spatial acuity, as measured via spatial gap detection, spatial gap identification, and the perception of high spatial frequencies are improved when participants attend to smaller outline shapes (designed to induce narrow attentional breadth), whereas magnocellular-mediated perceptual processes such as temporal acuity, as measured via temporal gap detection and temporal order judgements, and the perception of low spatial frequencies are unaffected by this manipulation (Goodhew & Edwards, 2016; Goodhew et al., 2017; Goodhew et al., 2016).

3.3.3 Modern Evidence for the Zoom-Lens Model

As described in section 3.2, more recent work has questioned the usage of outline (unfilled) shapes in the attempted manipulation of attentional breadth (Lawrence, Edwards, & Goodhew, 2020; Lawrence, Edwards, Talipski, et al., 2020). This is because such stimuli may induce an annulus of attention, rather than changing the scope of attentional breadth. This is important because most of the testing of these pathway-specific models have used this method. When inducers are used which compel the spread of attention across the entire region, instead of encouraging an annulus of attention, then a pattern consistent with a re-interpreted zoom-lens model is obtained. That is, when global motion or Glass patterns are used to manipulate attentional breadth, then *both* spatial and temporal acuity has been found to benefit from a narrow relative to a broad attentional breadth (Lawrence, Edwards, & Goodhew, 2020).

3.3.4 Future Directions in Model Development

At this point, it appears that the zoom-lens model does a good job of encapsulating the relationship between attentional breadth and low-level aspects of visual perception, such as spatial and temporal acuity. When the appropriate method for manipulating attentional breadth is used, it does not appear that there are pathway-specific effects of attentional breadth on visual perception. Instead, spatial and temporal acuity both benefit from a narrow attentional breadth. However, there are many more complex visual processes that do not conform to the predictions from the zoom-lens model. The zoom-lens model cannot explain why processes such as face and object perception and the processing of scene summary statistics appear to benefit from a broad rather than a narrow attentional breadth (although these findings will need to be revisited in light of the methodological recommendations made above). However, further theoretical development is required in this space. If this evidence holds up under renewed testing, then new theoretical models would need to explain both how for low-level visual acuity a zoom lens pattern is obtained, but how this benefit of a narrow attentional breadth can be qualitatively reversed for other processes, such as object perception. First, it is important to retest the existing evidence with methods that meet the criteria espoused in section 3.2. This will ensure that we have a true picture of how attentional breadth per se impacts the many and varied visual tasks that humans perform. For example, does face perception truly benefit from a broad versus narrow attentional breadth, when it is established the whole face is encompassed by both the broad and narrow focus, rather than the narrow focus excluding part of the face? Addressing such questions will provide a solid foundation for future theoretical development.

This renewed theoretical development in understanding attentional breadth and its consequences for different psychological processes will likely entail a focus on more complex aspects of perception than low-level visual acuity. In doing so, it is important that the knowledge of the zoom lens-type effects on low-level visual perception is controlled for or discounted from any observed effects on more complex visual processes. A cautionary tale of the danger of not doing so is illustrated in the work examining the impact of attentional breadth on emotional processing.

Gable and Harmon-Jones (2011) manipulated attentional breadth by having participants respond to either the global or local elements in a directed Navon task and then measured the N1 event-related potential (ERP) in response to images of appetitive stimuli (compared against neutral stimuli). These authors conceptualised the N1 as being associated with motivation. It was found that the N1 amplitude was larger in the local (small attentional breadth) than the global (large attentional breadth) condition. Gable and Harmon-Jones (2011) interpreted this as evidence that a narrow attentional breadth is associated with greater approach related motivation. The strength of the conclusions that can be drawn from such studies relies on how strong the evidence is that the ERP component operationalises the psychological process that the authors claim. Gable and Harmon-Jones (2011) cite some evidence to support this claim that the N1 reflects motivational factors, however, it is worth bearing in mind that the N1 is a relatively early component, and elsewhere has been attributed to more basic visual processes such as generic target identification (Vogel & Luck, 2000). According to the zoom-lens model, perceptual processing of targets – including emotionally-salient or evocative ones – would be reduced under a broad (versus narrow) attentional breadth. Therefore, it is possible that the reduced N1 amplitude in the broad attention condition was entirely a product of reduced low-level target-related perceptual processing, rather than anything selective regarding emotion or motivation.

These authors' follow-up work gives even more credence to a zoom lens based explanation of their ERP results. Gable and Harmon-Jones (2012) examined the effect of attentional breadth on the N1 ERP component in response to disgust versus neutral pictures. Here, they found that the differential N1 amplitude was present when participants narrowed their attentional breadth, whereas it was not when participants broadened their attentional breadth. The authors interpreted this in the context of highlighting how attentional breadth impacts *emotional* processing. However, since the evidence that the emotion-based manipulation (i.e., disgust versus neutral pictures) affected the outcome measure (i.e., N1 amplitude) only in the narrow condition, it cannot be ruled out that this demonstrates the already well known influence of attentional breadth on visual perceptual resolution, as captured by the zoom-lens model. That is, the targets (and, therefore, the category to which they belonged) were processed more effectively under the narrow attentional breadth, leading to robust N1 amplitudes which disappeared when attention was diffused in the broad attentional breadth condition. It cannot be discounted from this evidence alone that this effect would have occurred *irrespective* of the emotional content of the targets. In other words, there may have also been enhanced category processing for a neutral distinction, because *all* target-related processing and categorisation would be enhanced under a narrow attentional breadth. In future research examining the influence of attentional breadth on 'higher level' processes, it is important to establish that any effects are above and beyond that which can be explained by the zoom lens relationship for low-level perceptual processes.

3.4 Manipulating Attentional Breadth: Summary and Conclusions

This section has discussed the importance of careful operationalisation of attentional breadth. In particular, I have outlined some key principles to guide the design of future studies testing the effect of attentional breadth on visual perception and performance. The goal of these is to ensure that manipulations actually compel changes in the size of the attentional breadth, and not inadvertently other cognitive or attentional processes. In addition, I gave an overview of theoretical development in this area to date and highlighted where future development is required. In particular, while the zoom-lens model appears to be a strong candidate for understanding the impact of attentional breadth on relatively low-level visual processes such as spatial and temporal acuity, the existing evidence suggests that attentional breadth impacts other visual-cognitive processes in *qualitatively* different ways, and any new models introduced will need to be able to account for these differences. Future theoretical development will also need to pay due diligence to the methodological issues addressed in the first part of this section. Some of the existing empirical evidence does need to be retested with improved methods to ensure that we have a clear picture of the true impact of attentional breadth on performance, and not one that is contaminated and solely relates to other attentional processes, such as shifts of attention. This new evidence will provide a strong foundation from which to develop comprehensive models to help us understand how attentional breadth impacts visual task performance.

4 Exogenous Versus Endogenous Attention and How It Relates to Attentional Breadth

When it comes to the literature on *shifts* of attention, it is clear that there are key taxonomies of attention that serve as touchstones that are used to conceptualise, guide, and interpret research. One major such one is that between *exogenous* versus *endogenous* (see also bottom-up versus top-down; transient versus sustained, and involuntary versus voluntary) attentional orienting (Awh, Belopolsky, & Theeuwes, 2012). The taxonomy has already been explicitly referred to in the attentional breadth literature, for the purpose of resolving discrepant findings across different studies (Mounts & Edwards, 2017). This section will critically review and discuss the utility of this taxonomy for understanding attentional breadth.

Exogenous attentional orienting is considered to be a more automatic or reflexive form of orienting, typically elicited by peripherally presented stimuli. The orienting is said to occur rapidly due to the stimulus' physical salience, irrespective of the person's current task or goals. In contrast, endogenous attentional orienting is conceptualised as a more strategic or controlled form of orienting. This type of orienting is often elicited by centrally presented symbolic stimuli that are predictive of the location of target stimuli. Endogenous attentional orienting typically occurs on a longer timescale than exogenous attentional orienting (Awh et al., 2012; Chica, Bartolomeo, & Lupianez, 2013; Folk, Remington, & Johnston, 1992; Jonides, 1981; Posner, 1980; Posner et al., 1980). More recently, an additional category has been added to the taxonomy of attention, called *selection history*, which is said to encompass the forms of attentional orienting not captured by the top-down/bottom-up distinction (Awh et al., 2012; Kadel, Feldmann-Wustefeld, & Schubo, 2017; for an earlier version of this that was not named selection history but fits its contemporary definition; see Nakayama & Mackeben, 1989). However, for a discussion of its merits, see Hommel et al. (2019). Most importantly, selection history does not salvage the taxonomy from the critiques levelled here and does not clarify the application of the taxonomy to attentional breadth.

Is this attentional taxonomy a useful one for understanding attentional breadth? Is the distinction between exogenous and endogenous attention the reason that one study found no effect of attentional breadth on temporal resolution (Goodhew et al., 2016), while another found an improvement under broad, as suggested by Mounts and Edwards (2017)? There are a number of other differences between the methods of these studies (for a review, see Lawrence, Edwards, Talipski, et al., 2020). Is the distinction between exogenous and endogenous attention one that ought to be considered? Here I argue that before it can have value in understanding the process of regulating attentional breadth, there needs to be greater clarity and consensus about what this distinction means, and how it operationalised, with respect to shifts of attention.

For example, Yeshurun and colleagues have conducted some important work on the perceptual consequences of transient (contrasted with sustained) attention. This work has shown that when a transient peripheral cue is used, spatial resolution is enhanced while temporal resolution is impaired (Baruch & Yeshurun, 2014; Yeshurun & Levy, 2003; Yeshurun & Marom, 2008). In contrast, sustained attention has been found to benefit both spatial and temporal acuity (Hein, Rolke, & Ulrich, 2006; Yeshurun, Montagna, & Carrasco, 2008). While not specifically using the terms exogenous versus endogenous, this work does draw a distinction between a fast and slow form of attentional orienting, which maps onto the exogenous/endogenous distinction. However, in this light, the conclusions from this work appear to contrast sharply with the conclusions of other researchers, such as that only voluntarily (i.e., endogenously) shifted attention can impact visual perception for stimuli at the attended location, whereas involuntarily (i.e., exogenously) shifted attention cannot, and can only influence response efficiency (Prinzmetal et al., 2005; Prinzmetal, Zvinyatskovskiy, Gutierrez, & Dilem, 2009). Therefore, on one hand, there is the claim that visual perception is impacted by exogenous attentional shifts, whereas on the other there is the claim that visual perception is only impacted by endogenous shifts and not exogenous shifts.

The transient cueing paradigms used by Yeshurun et al. entailed a comparison between valid trials (peripheral cue that predicted the location of the target) versus neutral trials (either a central cue, which did not misdirect attention like an invalid cue, but rather just provided no spatial information about the upcoming peripheral target, or a cue appearing in every possible target location) (Chica

& Christie, 2009). There were no invalid trials. This means that the spatially informative peripheral cues were 100 per cent predictive. That is, every time a participant saw a single peripherally presented cue, it *always* appeared in the same location as the subsequent target. Therefore, here this transient peripheral cue is *predictive*, which is a characteristic that has been claimed to distinguish *endogenous*, rather than exogenous orienting. However, it also entails a peripheral cue and short cue–target interval, thought to be indicative of exogenous attentional orienting. Does this mean that the so-called transient attentional orienting paradigm used in these studies is a form of exogenous attentional orienting, endogenous attentional orienting, or some hybrid of the two? The answer to this ultimately depends on the relative weighting of the defining features of these categories. For example, if the timing is the single most important determinant, then we can consider this transient attentional orienting a form of exogenous attentional orienting. In contrast, if the predictive nature of the cue is critical, then it may compel us to reclassify transient attentional orienting as endogenous attentional orienting. In this vein, it is interesting that the apparent impairment for temporal acuity reported by Yeshurun et al. has been found to abolished when a comparison between valid and *invalid* trials is instead used, thereby undoing the predictiveness of the peripheral cue (Chica & Christie, 2009). Altogether, while predictiveness stands out as a candidate, it remains unknown whether the central/peripheral, slow/fast, or predictive/non-predictive distinction is the one that is truly defining of the exogenous versus endogenous distinction in relation to attentional shifts. This issue needs to be resolved before this taxonomy can have any utility in understanding different mechanisms of regulating attentional breadth.

In part, a clarifying solution to this muddiness will arise when researchers use terms in clear and consistent ways. At present, the majority of papers are silent on this when they adopt this terminology. I recommend that when authors say that they are studying exogenous or endogenous attentional orienting, they explicitly identify what characteristics have led them to adopt this definition. In addition to this, greater clarity will emerge from greater foundational work. In particular, what is required is to find a dependent variable that reliably distinguishes between 'hallmark' exogenous and endogenous attentional orienting (e.g., all three defining features used to make a textbook example of each type of attentional orienting). Then, each of these features should be varied systematically to determine when this marker of each type of orienting emerges. Prinzmetal et al. (Prinzmetal et al., 2005; Prinzmetal et al., 2009) have provided evidence that only predictive cues affect perception (i.e., accuracy), whereas non-predictive cues affect response efficiency (i.e., RT) but not accuracy. A foundational study could systematically vary the temporal interval between the cue and target, whether it is central or peripheral, and how predictive it is to determine when accuracy based cueing effects emerge, versus when they do not. Alternatively, a neuroimaging outcome variable could be used, since different neural regions have been implicated in different types of attentional orienting (Corbetta & Shulman, 2002; Shomstein, Lee, & Behrmann, 2010). Such work would help the field to understand whether one of these characteristics determines whether a qualitatively different pattern of consequences for the attentional orienting emerges (indicative of a distinct type of attentional orienting), or whether some combination of these is required. This would elucidate our understanding of what truly defines different types of attentional shifts.

From this discussion, it should be clear that greater foundational work is required in relation to understanding how this taxonomy relates to the orienting of attention before it can be usefully applied to understanding changes in the scale of attentional breadth. Moreover, even if we consider some of the likely candidates, which may turn out to differentiate different types of attentional orienting, it appears that some have a poor fit with attentional breadth. For example, in standard attention cueing studies, a cue and a target are presented on each trial. This means that it is simple to conceptualise what the time interval is between the cue and the target to quantify the speed of the orienting. However, attentional breadth can be manipulated by stimuli on different trials to the targets designed to gauge acuity. Quantifying cue–target interval is not straightforward in this case. The central versus peripheral distinction does not map cleanly onto attentional breadth, since in a well-designed study the stimuli manipulating attentional breadth should always be centrally presented, otherwise shifts and breadth changes are conflated (see Section 3). Even a dimension like predictiveness seems out-of-context when considering the induction of different attentional breadths. In a well-designed study, all performance–outcome targets will appear within the current attended region, all that would change is the current breadth-of-attention. There may be another distinction – such as whether or not a task is performed on the inducing stimuli – will turn out to produce different consequences of attentional breadth. In some paradigms, stimuli are merely presented (Benso et al., 1998; Mounts & Edwards, 2017), whereas in others active processing and a response is required (Chong & Treisman, 2005; Lawrence, Edwards, & Goodhew, 2020). This may turn out to be a meaningful distinction. However, this ought to be a data-driven distinction (e.g., studies that are identical in all respects except this one produce different patterns of results), rather than assumption driven.

Throughout the discussion in this section, I have made several assumptions, which I highlight here. If these assumptions turn out to be unfounded, then the resulting conclusion (i.e., that the exogenous/endogenous distinction is in such a state of confusion and misuse in the domain of shifts that it cannot be expected to offer any assistance in understanding attentional breadth, at least at this point), would be unchanged, or if anything, would provide even further justification for it. The first assumption I have made is that there is a meaningful exogenous versus endogenous distinction underlying all of the confusion and that this can be detected and clarified with further work. I think that this assumption is well founded, given there does appear to be meaningful dissociations observed in the literature (Prinzmetal et al., 2005), However, if it turns out that there is not a meaningful distinction underlying this, or there is but some other framework is found to have greater merit than the exogenous versus endogenous one in understanding it, then this would only further reinforce the inappropriateness of borrowing the exogenous/endogenous distinction in our mission to better understand attentional breadth. The second assumption is that I have talked about an exogenous versus endogenous distinction, implicitly invoking a categorical structure. It may be that rather than qualitatively distinct and mutually exclusive mechanisms, these two mechanisms are always at play and in tension, and observed instances of attentional orienting may reflect the preferential rather than absolute involvement of one versus the other. I have no issue with such a conceptualisation, indeed, it is common in cognitive psychology to see a shift from categorical to continuous conceptualisations as a field matures (e.g., rather than pre-attentive versus attentive, now we typically talk about degrees of efficiency in visual search). However, a more nuanced model such as this does not escape the requirement to identify the preference defining characteristics. This is similar to the magno/parvo distinction highlighted in Section 3: real-world visual processing is subserved by contributions from both of these pathways, but the stimulus properties which preferentially recruit one of these pathways are known, such that we know that very high temporal frequency stimuli and very high spatial frequency stimuli would be predominately resolved by the magnocellular versus parvocellular pathways. What are the attributes that determine preferential exogenous and endogenous contributions to attentional orienting? In the absence of a consensus answer to this question, this framework has little to offer in enhancing our understanding of attentional breadth.

To summarise, given the lack of clarity regarding the defining features of the exogenous versus endogenous distinction with respect to shifts of attention, this is unlikely to be a helpful taxonomy in understanding different mechanisms of changing or setting the breadth-of-attention at this time. Instead, whether there are indeed different types of attentional breadth changes is a conclusion that ultimately needs to be determined by carefully controlled experiments, rather than something that is assumed at the outset. In other words, it will be unproductive for the terms 'exogenous' and 'endogenous' to be used loose and fast for attentional breadth and could cause unnecessary confusion, as it arguably has for attentional shifts.

5 Conclusions

Humans can focus their attention narrowly (e.g., to read this text) or broadly (e.g., to determine which way a large crowd of people is moving). This is attentional breadth. Section 2 of this Element described a subset of the litany of laboratory tasks that refer, either implicitly or explicitly, to attentional breadth or a related concept, and claim to measure it. While there is a minimal explicit discussion of meaningful subcomponents of attentional breadth in the literature, a survey of the available evidence suggests that there may be some important distinctions, such as attentional breadth control versus attentional breadth preference. Offering more formal proposals regarding the structure of attention breadth (i.e., the meaningful divisions of sub-processes) and submitting them to rigorous testing, and refining them in light of new evidence, promises to be a productive avenue forward. Section 2 provided a road map of some of the key conceptual and methodological issues to address in traversing these avenues forward. In other words, I highlighted some of the psychometric criteria that I believe ought to be considered in assessing the validity of measures of attentional breadth and hypothesised underlying architecture of attentional breadth processes.

Attentional breadth appears to impact many other aspects of visual perception and cognition, and Section 3 considered these consequences of attentional breadth. In doing so, I explained five key methodological criteria that are important to consider when experimentally manipulating attentional breadth, to ensure that other attentional processes (e.g., shifts) are not inadvertently manipulated instead of, or as well as, attentional breadth. In Section 3, I also reviewed the existing theoretical accounts and discussed where they fall short in accounting for the available evidence. I discussed potential avenues forward for theoretical development. But a word of caution: the methodological issues which affect some of the earlier work on attentional breadth means that we may not have a true understanding of its consequences for visual task performance. Therefore, a necessary next step is to rigorously test the effect of attentional breadth using new innovative procedures (e.g., the global motion approach) that address the issues with existing techniques. This will provide a strong foundation for theoretical development.

Section 5 critically evaluated the utility of the exogenous/endogenous distinction from the shifts literature to understanding attentional breadth. The overarching point here was that without a clear consensus regarding the defining properties of these categories in relation to shifts, it has little utility in improving our understanding of attentional breadth, and in fact carries a considerable risk of confusing rather than illuminating. The justification for any distinction in relation to attentional breadth should be bolstered by evidence, not assumptions.

Given the importance of attentional breadth to many aspects of human functioning, addressing the issues I raised here and advancing the science in this area promises to provide important practical benefits in addition to a satisfying theoretical understanding.

References

Ahmed, L., & de Fockert, J. W. (2012). Focusing on Attention: The Effects of Working Memory Capacity and Load on Selective Attention. *Plos One, 7*(8), e43101. doi:10.1371/journal.pone.0043101

Awh, E., Belopolsky, A. V., & Theeuwes, J. (2012). Top-down versus bottom-up attentional control: A failed theoretical dichotomy. *Trends in Cognitive Sciences, 16*(8), 437–43. doi:10.1016/j.tics.2012.06.010

Badcock, J. C., Whitworth, F. A., Badcock, D. R., & Lovegrove, W. J. (1990). Low-frequency filtering and the processing of local-global stimuli. *Perception, 19*(5), 617–29. doi:10.1068/p190617

Baddeley, A. (2012). Working memory: Theories, models, and controversies. *Annual Review of Psychology, 63* (1), 1–29. doi:10.1146/annurev-psych-120710-100422

Baddeley, A., & Hitch, G. J. (1974). Working memory. In G. A. Bower ed., *The Psychology of Learning and Motivation*, 8, 47–89: New York: Academic Press.

Ball, K., Beard, B. L., Roenker, D. L., Miller, R. L., & Griggs, D. S. (1988). Age and visual search: expanding the useful field of view. *Journal of the Optical Society of America, A, Optics, Image Science & Vision, 5*(12), 2210–19.

Ball, K., Owsley, C., Sloane, M. E., Roenker, D. L., & Bruni, J. R. (1993). Visual attention problems as a predictor of vehicle crashes in older drivers. *Investigative Opthalmology & Visual Sciences, 34*(11), 3110–23.

Balz, G. W., & Hock, H. S. (1997). The effect of attentional spread on spatial resolution. *Vision Research, 37*(11), 1499–510. doi:10.1016/S0042-6989(96)00296-9

Bar, M., Kassam, K. S., Ghuman, A. S., Boshyan, J., Schmidt, A. M., Dale, A. M.,... Halgren, E. (2006). Top-down facilitation of visual recognition. *Proceedings of the National Academy of Sciences, 103*(2), 449–54. doi:10.1073/pnas.0507062103

Bar-Haim, Y., Lamy, D., Pergamin, L., Bakermans-Kranenburg, M. J., & van Ijzendoorn, M. H. (2007). Threat-related attentional bias in anxious and nonanxious individuals: A meta-analytic study. *Psychological Bulletin, 133* (1), 1–24. doi:10.1037/0033-2909.133.1.1

Baruch, O., & Yeshurun, Y. (2014). Attentional attraction of receptive fields can explain spatial and temporal effects of attention. *Visual Cognition, 22*(5), 704–36. doi:10.1080/13506285.2014.911235

Basso, M. R., Schefft, B. K., Ris, M. D., & Dember, W. N. (1996). Mood and global-local visual processing. *Journal of the International Neuropsychological Society, 2*(3), 249–55. doi:10.1017/S1355617700001193

Baumann, N., & Kuhl, J. (2005). Positive Affect and Flexibility: Overcoming the Precedence of Global over Local Processing of Visual Information. *Motivation and Emotion, 29*(2), 123–34. doi:10.1007/s11031-005-7957-1

Behrmann, M., Avidan, G., Leonard, G. L., Kimchi, R., Luna, B., Humphreys, K., & Minshew, N. (2006). Configural processing in autism and its relationship to face processing. *Neuropsychologia, 44*(1), 110–29. doi:10.1016/j.neuropsychologia.2005.04.002

Belopolsky, A. V., Zwaan, L., Theeuwes, J., & Kramer, A. F. (2007). The size of an attentional window modulates attentional capture by color singletons. *Psychonomic Bulletin & Review, 14*(5), 934–8. doi:10.3758/bf03194124

Bennett, P. J., & Pratt, J. (2001). The spatial distribution of inhibition of return. *Psychological Science, 12*(1), 76–80. doi:10.1111/1467-9280.00313

Benso, F., Turatto, B., & Gastone, G. (1998). The time course of attentional focusing. *European Journal of Cognitive Psychology, 10*(4), 373–88. doi:10.1080/713752283

Biggs, A. T., & Gibson, B. S. (2018). Opening the window: Size of the attentional window dominates perceptual load and familiarity in visual selection. *Journal of Experimental Psychology: Human Perception & Performance, 44*(11), 1780–98. doi:10.1037/xhp0000565

Bleckley, M. K., Durso, F. T., Crutchfield, J. M., Engle, R. W., & Khanna, M. M. (2003). Individual differences in working memory capacity predict visual attention allocation. *Psychonomic Bulletin & Review, 10*(4), 884–9. doi:10.3758/BF03196548

Bocanegra, B. R., & Zeelenberg, R. (2011). Emotion-induced trade-offs in spatiotemporal vision. *Journal of Experimental Psychology: General, 140* (2), 272–82. doi:10.1037/a0023188

Brown, T. A., Chorpita, B. F., Korotitsch, W., & Barlow, D. H. (1997). Psychometric properties of the Depression Anxiety Stress Scales (DASS) in clinical samples. *Behav Res Ther, 35*(1), 79–89. doi:10.1016/S0005-7967(96)00068-X

Bruyer, R., & Brysaert, M. (2011). Combining speed and accuracy in cognitive psychology: Is the inverse efficiency score (IES) a better dependent variable than the mean reaction time (RT) and the percentage of errors (PE)? *Psychologica Belgica, 51*(1), 5–13. doi:10.5334/pb-51-1-5

Buetti, S., Lleras, A., & Moore, C. M. (2014). The flanker effect does not reflect the processing of "task-irrelevant" stimuli: evidence from inattentional blindness. *Psychonomic Bulletin & Review, 21*(5), 1231–37. doi:10.3758/s13423-014-0602-9

Bulakowski, P. F., Bressler, D. W., & Whitney, D. (2007). Shared attentional resources for global and local motion processing. *Journal of Vision, 7*(10), 1–10 doi:10.1167/7.10.10

Burr, D. C., Concetta Morrone, M., & Vaina, L. M. (1998). Large receptive fields for optic flow detection in humans. *Vision Research, 38*(12), 1731–43. doi:10.1016/S0042-6989(97)00346-5

Bush, W. S., & Vecera, S. P. (2014). Differential effect of one versus two hands on visual processing. *Cognition, 133*(1), 232–7. doi:10.1016/j.cognition.2014.06.014

Calcott, R. D., & Berkman, E. T. (2014). Attentional Flexibility During Approach and Avoidance Motivational States: The Role of Context in Shifts of Attentional Breadth. *Journal of Experimental Psychology: General, 143*(3), 1393–408. doi:10.1037/a0035060

Caparos, S., & Linnell, K. J. (2010). The spatial focus of attention is controlled at perceptual and cognitive levels. *Journal of Experimental Psychology: Human Perception and Performance, 36*(5), 1080–107. doi:10.1037/a0020367

Caparos, S., Linnell, K. J., Bremner, A. J., de Fockert, J. W., & Davidoff, J. (2013). Do local and global perceptual biases tell us anything about local and global selective attention? *Psychological Science, 24*(2), 206–12. doi:10.1177/0956797612452569

Carrasco, M. (2011). Visual attention: The past 25 years. *Vision Research, 51*(13), 1484–525. doi:10.1016/j.visres.2011.04.012

Castiello, U., & Umiltà, C. (1990). Size of the attentional focus and efficiency of processing. *Acta Psychologica, 73*(3), 195–209. doi:10.1016/0001-6918(90)90022-8

Chica, A. B., Bartolomeo, P., & Lupianez, J. (2013). Two cognitive and neural systems for endogenous and exogenous spatial attention. *Behavioural Brain Research, 237*, 107–23. doi:10.1016/j.bbr.2012.09.027

Chica, A. B., & Christie, J. (2009). Spatial attention does improve temporal discrimination. *Attention, Perception, & Psychophysics, 71*(2), 273–80. doi:10.3758/APP.71.2.273

Chong, S. C., & Treisman, A. (2005). Attentional spread in the statistical processing of visual displays. *Perception & Psychophysics, 67*(1), 1–13. doi:10.3758/bf03195009

Corbetta, M., & Shulman, G. L. (2002). Control of goal-directed and stimulus-driven attention in the brain. *Nature Reviews Neuroscience, 3*(3), 201–15. doi:10.1038/nrn755

Corbetta, M., & Shulman, G. L. (2011). Spatial neglect and attention networks. *Annual Review of Neuroscience, 34,* 569–99. doi:10.1146/annurev-neuro-061010-113731

Coren, S., Ward, L. M., & Enns, J. T. (2004). *Sensation and Perception*: New York: J. Wiley & Sons.

Cosman, J. D., Lees, M. N., Lee, J. D., Rizzo, M., & Vecera, S. P. (2012). Impaired attentional disengagement in older adults with useful field of view decline. *The Journals of Gerontology, Series B: Psychological Sciences and Social Sciences, 67*(4), 405–12. doi:10.1093/geronb/gbr116

Cox, J. A., Christensen, B. K., & Goodhew, S. C. (2018). Temporal dynamics of anxiety-related attentional bias: Is affective context a missing piece of the puzzle? *Cognition & emotion, 32*(6), 1329–38. doi:10.1080/02699931.2017.1386619

Cutzu, F., & Tsotsos, J. K. (2003). The selective tuning model of attention: psychophysical evidence for a suppressive annulus around an attended item. *Vision Research, 43*(2), 205–19. doi:10.1016/s0042-6989(02)00491-1

Dale, G., & Arnell, K. M. (2013). Investigating the stability of and relationships among global/local processing measures. *Attention, Perception & Psychophysics, 75*(3), 394–406. doi:10.3758/s13414-012-0416-7

Dale, G., & Arnell, K. M. (2015). Multiple measures of dispositional global/local bias predict attentional blink magnitude. *Psychological Research, 79*(4), 534–47. doi:10.1007/s00426-014-0591-3

Delchau, H. L., Christensen, B. K., O'Kearney, R., & Goodhew, S. C. (2019). What is top-down about seeing enemies? Social anxiety and attention to threat. *Attention, Perception, & Psychophysics.* doi:10.3758/s13414-019-01920-3

Dell'Acqua, R., Dux, P. E., Wyble, B., Doro, M., Sessa, P., Meconi, F., & Jolicoeur, P. (2015). The attentional blink impairs detection and delays encoding of visual information: evidence from human electrophysiology. *Journal of Cognitive Neuroscience, 27*(4), 720–35. doi:10.1162/jocn_a_00752

Denison, R. N., Vu, A. T., Yacoub, E., Feinberg, D. A., & Silver, M. A. (2014). Functional mapping of the magnocellular and parvocellular subdivisions of human LGN. *NeuroImage, 2,* 358–69. doi:10.1016/j.neuroimage.2014.07.019

Derrington, A. M., & Lennie, P. (1984). Spatial and temporal contrast sensitivities of neurones in the lateral geniculate nucleus of the macaque. *Journal of Physiology, 357,* 219–40.

Downing, C. J. (1988). Expectancy and visual-spatial attention: Effects on perceptual quality. *Journal of Experimental Psychology: Human*

Perception and Performance, 14(2), 188–202. doi:10.1037/0096-1523.14.2.188

Edwards, J. D., Fausto, B. A., Tetlow, A. M., Corona, R. T., & Valdes, E. G. (2018). Systematic review and meta-analyses of useful field of view cognitive training. *Neuroscience & Biobehavioral Reviews, 84,* 72–91. doi:10.1016/j.neubiorev.2017.11.004

Enns, J. T., & Akhtar, N. (1989). A developmental study of filtering in visual attention. *Child Dev, 60*(5), 1188–99. doi:10.2307/1130792

Enns, J. T., & Girgus, J. S. (1985). Developmental changes in selective and integrative visual attention. *Journal of Experimental Child Psychology, 40* (2), 319–37. doi:10.1016/0022-0965(85)90093-1

Enns, J. T., & Kingstone, A. (1995). Access to Global and Local Properties in Visual Search for Compound Stimuli. *Psychological Science, 6*(5), 283–91. doi:10.1111/j.1467-9280.1995.tb00512.x

Eriksen, B. A., & Eriksen, C. W. (1974). Effects of noise letters upon the identification of a target letter in a nonsearch task. *Perception & Psychophysics, 16*(1), 143–9. doi:10.3758/bf03203267

Eriksen, C. W., & St. James, J. D. (1986). Visual attention within and around the field of focal attention: A zoom lens model. *Perception & Psychophysics, 40* (4), 225–40. doi:10.3758/BF03211502

Fan, J., McCandliss, B. D., Fossella, J., Flombaum, J. I., & Posner, M. I. (2005). The activation of attentional networks. *NeuroImage, 26*(2), 471–9. doi:10.1016/j.neuroimage.2005.02.004

Fang, L., Hoorelbeke, K., Bruyneel, L., Notebaert, L., MacLeod, C., De Raedt, R., & Koster, E. H. (2017). Can training change attentional breadth? Failure to find transfer effects. *Psychological Research, 82*(3), 520–34. doi:10.1007/s00426-017-0845-y

Fang, L., Sanchez-Lopez, A., & Koster, E. H. W. (2018). Attentional scope, rumination, and processing of emotional information: An eye-tracking study. *Emotion, 19* (7), 1257–67. doi:10.1037/emo0000516

Fenske, M. J., & Eastwood, J. D. (2003). Modulation of focused attention by faces expressing emotion: evidence from flanker tasks. *Emotion, 3*(4), 327–43. doi:10.1037/1528-3542.3.4.327

Ferrera, V. P., Nealey, T. A., & Maunsell, J. R. (1992). Mixed parvocellular and magnocellular geniculate signals in visual area V4. *Nature, 358,* 756–8. doi:10.1038/358756a0

Folk, C. L., Remington, R. W., & Johnston, J. C. (1992). Involuntary covert orienting is contingent on attentional control settings. *Journal of Experimental Psychology: Human Perception & Performance, 18*(4), 1030–44. doi:10.1037/0096-1523.18.4.1030

Fredrickson, B. L., & Branigan, C. (2005). Positive emotions broaden the scope of attention and thought-action repertoires. *Cognition and Emotion, 19*(3), 313–32. doi:10.1080/02699930441000238

Gable, P. A., & Harmon-Jones, E. (2008). Approach-motivated positive affect reduces breadth of attention. *Psychological Science, 19*(5), 476–82. doi:10.1111/j.1467-9280.2008.02112.x

Gable, P. A., & Harmon-Jones, E. (2010a). The blues broaden, but the nasty narrows: attentional consequences of negative affects low and high in motivational intensity. *Psychological Science, 21*(2), 211–15. doi:10.1177/0956797609359622

Gable, P. A., & Harmon-Jones, E. (2010b). The effect of low versus high approach-motivated positive affect on memory for peripherally versus centrally presented information. *Emotion, 10*(4), 599–603. doi:10.1037/a0018426

Gable, P. A., & Harmon-Jones, E. (2011). Attentional states influence early neural responses associated with motivational processes: local vs. global attentional scope and N1 amplitude to appetitive stimuli. *Biological Psychology, 87*(2), 303–5. doi:10.1016/j.biopsycho.2011.02.007

Gable, P. A., & Harmon-Jones, E. (2012). Reducing attentional capture of emotion by broadening attention: increased global attention reduces early electrophysiological responses to negative stimuli. *Biological Psychology, 90*(2), 150–3. doi:10.1016/j.biopsycho.2012.02.006

Gao, Z., Flevaris, A. V., Robertson, L. C., & Bentin, S. (2011). Priming global and local processing of composite faces: revisiting the processing-bias effect on face perception. *Attention, Perception & Psychophysics, 73*(5), 1477–86. doi:10.3758/s13414-011-0109-7

Gasper, K., & Clore, G. L. (2002). Attending to the big picture: mood and global versus local processing of visual information. *Psychological Science, 13*(1), 34–40. doi:10.1111/1467-9280.00406

Gerlach, C., & Starrfelt, R. (2018). Global precedence effects account for individual differences in both face and object recognition performance. *Psychonomic Bulletin & Review, 25*(4), 1365–72. doi:10.3758/s13423-018-1458-1

Goodale, M. A., & Milner, A. D. (1992). Separate visual pathways for perception and action. *Trends in Neurosciences, 15*(1), 20–5. doi:10.1016/0166-2236(92)90344-8

Goodhew, S. C. (2017). What have we learned from two decades of object-substitution masking? Time to update: Object individuation prevails over substitution. *Journal of Experimental Psychology: Human Perception and Performance, 43*(6), 1249–62. doi:10.1037/xhp0000395

Goodhew, S. C., & Clarke, R. (2016). Contributions of parvocellular and magnocellular pathways to visual perception near the hands are not fixed, but can be dynamically altered. *Psychonomic Bulletin & Review*, *23*(1), 156–62. doi:10.3758/s13423-015-0844-1

Goodhew, S. C., Dawel, A., & Edwards, M. (2020). Standardizing measurement in psychological studies: On why one second has different value in a sprint versus a marathon. *Behavior Research Methods*. doi:10.3758/s13428-020-01383-7

Goodhew, S. C., & Edwards, M. (2016). Object individuation is invariant to attentional diffusion: Changes in the size of the attended region do not interact with object-substitution masking. *Cognition*, *157*, 358–64. doi:10.1016/j.cognition.2016.10.006

Goodhew, S. C., & Edwards, M. (2019). Translating experimental paradigms into individual-differences research: Contributions, challenges, and practical recommendations. *Consciousness and Cognition*, *69*, 14–25. doi:10.1016/j.concog.2019.01.008

Goodhew, S. C., Edwards, M., Ferber, S., & Pratt, J. (2015). Altered visual perception near the hands: A critical review of attentional and neurophysiological models. *Neuroscience & Biobehavioral Reviews*, *55*, 223–33. doi:10.1016/j.neubiorev.2015.05.006

Goodhew, S. C., Lawrence, R. K., & Edwards, M. (2017). Testing the generality of the zoom-lens model: Evidence for visual-pathway specific effects of attended-region size on perception. *Attention, Perception & Psychophysics*, *79*(4), 1147–64. doi:10.3758/s13414-017-1306-9

Goodhew, S. C., & Plummer, A. S. (2019). Flexibility in resizing attentional breadth: Asymmetrical versus symmetrical attentional contraction and expansion costs depends on context. *Quarterly Journal of Experimental Psychology*, *72*(10), 2527–40. doi:10.1177/1747021819846831

Goodhew, S. C., Shen, E., & Edwards, M. (2016). Selective spatial enhancement: Attentional spotlight size impacts spatial but not temporal perception. *Psychonomic Bulletin & Review*, *23*(4), 1144–9. doi:10.3758/s13423-015-0904-6

Gozli, D. G., West, G. L., & Pratt, J. (2012). Hand position alters vision by biasing processing through different visual pathways. *Cognition*, *124*(2), 244–50. doi:10.1016/j.cognition.2012.04.008

Greene, M. R., & Oliva, A. (2009). The briefest of glances: The time course of natural scene understanding. *Psychological Science*, *20*(4), 464–72. doi:10.1111/j.1467-9280.2009.02316.x

Greenwood, P., & Parasuraman, R. (1999). Scale of attentional focus in visual search. *Perception & Psychophysics*, *61*(5), 837–59. doi:10.3758/BF03206901

Greenwood, P., & Parasuraman, R. (2004). The scaling of spatial attention in visual search and its modification in healthy aging. *Perception & Psychophysics, 66*(1), 3–22. doi:10.3758/BF03194857

Gu, L., Yang, X., Li, L. M. W., Zhou, X., & Gao, D. G. (2017). Seeing the big picture: Broadening attention relieves sadness and depressed mood. *Scandinavian Journal of Psychology, 58*(4), 324–32. doi:10.1111/sjop.12376

Hanif, A., Ferrey, A. E., Frischen, A., Pozzobon, K., Eastwood, J. D., Smilek, D., & Fenske, M. J. (2012). Manipulations of attention enhance self-regulation. *Acta Psychologica, 139*(1), 104–10. doi:10.1016/j.actpsy.2011.09.010

Hedge, C., Powell, G., & Sumner, P. (2018). The reliability paradox: Why robust cognitive tasks do not produce reliable individual differences. *Behavior Research Methods, 50*(3), 1166–86. doi:10.3758/s13428-017-0935-1

Hein, E., Rolke, B., & Ulrich, R. (2006). Visual attention and temporal discrimination: Differential effects of automatic and voluntary cueing. *Visual Cognition, 13*(1), 29–50. doi:10.1080/13506280500143524

Heitz, R. P., & Engle, R. W. (2007). Focusing the spotlight: individual differences in visual attention control. *Journal of Experimental Psychology: General, 136*(2), 217–40. doi:10.1037/0096-3445.136.2.217

Hoar, S., & Linnell, K. J. (2013). Cognitive load eliminates the global perceptual bias for unlimited exposure durations. *Attention, Perception, & Psychophysics, 75*(2), 210–15. doi:10.3758/s13414-012-0421-x

Hock, H. S., Park, C. L., & Schoner, G. (2002). Self-organized pattern formation: experimental dissection of motion detection and motion integration by variation of attentional spread. *Vision Research, 42*(8), 991–1003. doi:10.1016/S0042-6989(02)00026-3

Hommel, B., Chapman, C. S., Cisek, P., Neyedli, H. F., Song, J.-H., & Welsh, T. N. (2019). No one knows what attention is. *Attention, Perception, & Psychophysics, 81*(7), 2288–303. doi:10.3758/s13414-019-01846-w

Hotton, M., Derakshan, N., & Fox, E. (2018). A randomised controlled trial investigating the benefits of adaptive working memory training for working memory capacity and attentional control in high worriers. *Behav Res Ther, 100*, 67–77. doi:10.1016/j.brat.2017.10.011

Hubner, R. (2000). Attention shifting between global and local target levels: The persistence of level-repetition effects. *Visual Cognition, 7*(4), 465–84. doi:10.1080/135062800394612

Huttermann, S., Bock, O., & Memmert, D. (2012). The breadth of attention in old age. *Ageing Research, 3*(1), 67–70. doi:doi.org/10.4081/ar.2012.e10

Huttermann, S., & Memmert, D. (2015). The influence of motivational and mood states on visual attention: A quantification of systematic differences and casual changes in subjects' focus of attention. *Cognition & emotion, 29* (3), 471–83. doi:10.1080/02699931.2014.920767

Huttermann, S., & Memmert, D. (2018). Effects of lab- and field-based attentional training on athletes' attention-window. *Psychology of Sport and Exercise, 38*, 17–27. doi:10.1016/j.psychsport.2018.05.009

Huttermann, S., Memmert, D., & Simons, D. J. (2014). The size and shape of the attentional "spotlight" varies with differences in sports expertise. *Journal of Experimental Psychology: Applied, 20*(2), 147–57. doi:10.1037/xap0000012

Iacoviello, B. M., Wu, G., Abend, R., Murrough, J. W., Feder, A., Fruchter, E.,... Charney, D. S. (2014). Attention bias variability and symptoms of posttraumatic stress disorder. *J Trauma Stress, 27*(2), 232–9. doi:10.1002/jts.21899

Jefferies, L. N., & Di Lollo, V. (2015). When can spatial attention be deployed in the form of an annulus? *Attention, Perception, & Psychophysics, 77*(2), 413–22. doi:10.3758/s13414-014-0790-4

Jonides, J. (1981). Voluntary versus automatic control over the mind's eye's movement. In J. B. Long & A. D. Baddeley, eds., *Attention and Performance IX*. Hillsdale, New Jersey: Lawrence Erlbaum Associates. 187–203

Kadel, H., Feldmann-Wustefeld, T., & Schubo, A. (2017). Selection history alters attentional filter settings persistently and beyond top-down control. *Psychophysiology, 54*(5), 736–54. doi:10.1111/psyp.12830

Kimchi, R., & Palmer, S. E. (1982). Form and texture in hierarchically constructed patterns. *Journal of Experimental Psychology: Human Perception and Performance, 8*(4), 521–35. doi:10.1037//0096-1523.8.4.521

Kinchla, R. A., & Wolfe, J. M. (1979). The order of visual processing: "Top-down," "bottom-up," or "middle-out". *Perception & Psychophysics, 25*(3), 225–31. doi:10.3758/bf03202991

Klein, R. M. (2000). Inhibition of return. *Trends in Cognitive Sciences, 4*(4), 138–47. doi:10.1016/S1364-6613(00)01452-2

Koldewyn, K., Jiang, Y., Weigelt, S., & Kanwisher, N. (2013). Global/Local Processing in Autism: Not a Disability, but a Disinclination. *Journal of autism and developmental disorders, 43*(10), 2329–40. doi:10.1007/s10803-013-1777-z

Kosslyn, S. M., Brown, H. D., & Dror, I. E. (1999). Aging and the scope of visual attention. *Gerontology, 45*(2), 102–9. doi:10.1159/000022071

Koster, E. H., Crombez, G., Verschuere, B., Van Damme, S., & Wiersema, J. R. (2006). Components of attentional bias to threat in high trait anxiety:

Facilitated engagement, impaired disengagement, and attentional avoidance. *Behav Res Ther, 44*(12), 1757–71. doi:10.1016/j.brat.2005.12.011

Kramer, J. H., Ellenberg, L., Leonard, J., & Share, L. J. (1996). Developmental sex differences in global-local perceptual bias. *Neuropsychology, 10*(3), 402–7. doi:10.1037/0894-4105.10.3.402

Kreitz, C., Furley, P., Memmert, D., & Simons, D. J. (2015). Working-memory performance is related to spatial breadth of attention. *Psychological Research, 79*(6), 1034–41. doi:10.1007/s00426-014-0633-x

LaBerge, D. (1983). Spatial extent of attention to letters and words. *Journal of Experimental Psychology: Human Perception and Performance, 9*(3), 371–9. doi:10.1037/0096-1523.9.3.371

Lavie, N. (1995). Perceptual load as a necessary condition for selective attention. *Journal of Experimental Psychology: Human Perception and Performance, 21*(3), 451–68. doi:10.1037/0096-1523.21.3.451

Lavie, N. (2005). Distracted and confused?: Selective attention under load. *Trends in Cognitive Sciences, 9*(2), 75–82. doi:10.1016/j.tics.2004.12.004

Lawrence, R. K., Edwards, M., Chan, G. W. C., Cox, J. A., & Goodhew, S. C. (2019). Does cultural background predict the spatial distribution of attention? *Culture and Brain.* doi:10.1007/s40167-019-00086-x

Lawrence, R. K., Edwards, M., & Goodhew, S. C. (2018). Changes in the spatial spread of attention with ageing. *Acta Psychologica, 188,* 188–99. doi:10.1016/j.actpsy.2018.06.009

Lawrence, R. K., Edwards, M., & Goodhew, S. C. (2020). The impact of scaling rather than shaping attention: Changes in the scale of attention using global motion inducers influence both spatial and temporal acuity. *Journal of Experimental Psychology: Human Perception and Performance, 46*(3) 313–23.doi:10.1037/xhp0000708

Lawrence, R. K., Edwards, M. E., Talipski, L. A., & Goodhew, S. C. (2020). A critical review of the cognitive and perceptual factors influencing attentional scaling and visual processing. *Psychonomic Bulletin and Review.* doi:10.3758/s13423-019-01692-9

Leber, A. B., & Irons, J. L. (2019). A methodological toolbox for investigating attentional strategy. *Current Opinion in Psychology, 29,* 274–81. doi:10.1016/j.copsyc.2019.08.008

Livingstone, M., & Hubel, D. (1988). Segregation of form, color, movement, and depth: Anatomy, physiology, and perception. *Science, 240*(4853), 740–9. doi:10.1126/science.3283936

Lovibond, P. F., & Lovibond, S. H. (1995). The structure of negative emotional states: Comparison of the Depression Anxiety Stress Scales (DASS) with the

Beck Depression and Anxiety Inventories. *Behav Res Ther*, *33*(3), 335–43. doi:10.1016/0005-7967(94)00075-U

MacLeod, C., & Clarke, P. J. F. (2015). The Attentional Bias Modification Approach to Anxiety Intervention. *Clinical Psychological Science*, *3*(1), 58–78. doi:10.1177/2167702614560749

MacLeod, C., Grafton, B., & Notebaert, L. (2019). Anxiety-Linked Attentional Bias: Is It Reliable? *Annu Rev Clin Psychol*, *15*(1), 529–54. doi:10.1146/annurev-clinpsy-050718-095505

MacLeod, C., Mathews, A., & Tata, P. (1986). Attentional bias in emotional disorders. *Journal of Abnormal Psychology*, *95*(1), 15–20. doi:10.1037//0021-843x.95.1.15

Macrae, C. N., & Lewis, H. L. (2002). Do I know you? Processing orientation and face recognition. *Psychological Science*, *13*(2), 194–6. doi:10.1111/1467-9280.00436

McKone, E., Davies, A. A., Fernando, D., Aalders, R., Leung, H., Wickramariyaratne, T., & Platow, M. J. (2010). Asia has the global advantage: Race and visual attention. *Vision Research*, *50*(16), 1540–9. doi:10.1016/j.visres.2010.05.010

Milne, E., & Szczerbinski, M. (2009). Global and local perceptual style, field-independence, and central coherence: An attempt at concept validation. *Advances in Cognitive Psychology*, *5*, 1–26. doi:10.2478/v10053-008-0062-8

Mishkin, M., Ungerleider, L. G., & Macko, K. A. (1983). Object vision and spatial vision: Two cortical pathways. *Trends in Neurosciences*, *6*(10), 414–17. doi:10.1016/0166-2236(88)2990190-X

Moriya, J. (2018). Attentional networks and visuospatial working memory capacity in social anxiety. *Cognition and Emotion*, *32*(1), 158–66. doi:10.1080/02699931.2016.1263601

Most, S. B., Chun, M. M., Widders, D. M., & Zald, D. H. (2005). Attentional rubbernecking: Cognitive control and personality in emotion-induced blindness. *Psychonomic Bulletin & Review*, *12*(4), 654–61. doi:10.3758/BF03196754

Most, S. B., Smith, S. D., Cooter, A. B., Levy, B. N., & Zald, D. H. (2007). The naked truth: Positive, arousing distractors impair rapid target perception. *Cognition and Emotion*, *21*, 964–81. doi:10.1080/02699930600959340

Mounts, J. R. W. (2000a). Attentional capture by abrupt onsets and feature singletons produces inhibitory surrounds. *Perception & Psychophysics*, *62*(7), 1485–93. doi:10.3758/bf03212148

Mounts, J. R. W. (2000b). Evidence for suppressive mechanisms in attentional selection: Feature singletons produce inhibitory surrounds. *Perception & Psychophysics*, *62*(5), 969–83. doi:10.3758/bf03212082

Mounts, J. R. W., & Edwards, A. A. (2016). Attentional breadth and trade-offs in spatial and temporal acuity. *Visual Cognition*, 24(7–8), 422–33. doi:10.1080/13506285.2017.1294637

Muller, M., Malinowski, P., Gruber, T., & Hillyard, S. (2003). Sustained division of the attentional spotlight. *Nature*, 424(6946), 309–12. doi:10.1038/nature01812

Muller, N. G., Bartelt, O. A., Donner, T. H., Villringer, A., & Brandt, S. A. (2003). A physiological correlate of the "zoom lens" of visual attention. *Journal of Neuroscience*, 23(9), 3561–5. doi:10.1523/JNEUROSCI.23-09-03561.2003

Müller, N. G., Mollenhauer, M., Rösler, A., & Kleinschmidt, A. (2005). The attentional field has a Mexican hat distribution. *Vision Research*, 45(9), 1129–37. doi:10.1016/j.visres.2004.11.003

Najmi, S., Hindash, A. C., & Amir, N. (2010). Executive control of attention in individuals with contamination-related obsessive-compulsive symptoms. *Depression and anxiety*, 27(9), 807–12. doi:10.1002/da.20703

Nakayama, K., & Mackeben, M. (1989). Sustained and transient components of focal visual attention. *Vision Research*, 29(11), 1631–47. doi:10.1016/0042-6989(89)90144-2

Navon, D. (1977). Forest before trees: The precedence of global features in visual perception. *Cognitive Psychology*, 9(3), 353–83. doi:10.1016/0010-0285(77)90012-3

Navon, D. (1981). The forest revisited: More on global precedence. *Psychological Research*, 43(1), 1–32. doi:10.1007/bf00309635

Notebaert, L., Crombez, G., Van Damme, S., Durnez, W., & Theeuwes, J. (2013). Attentional prioritisation of threatening information: Examining the role of the size of the attentional window. *Cognition and Emotion*, 27(4), 621–31. doi:10.1080/02699931.2012.730036

Onie, S., & Most, S. B. (2017). Two roads diverged: Distinct mechanisms of attentional bias differentially predict negative affect and persistent negative thought. *Emotion*, 17(5), 884–94. doi:10.1037/emo0000280

Owsley, C. (2011). Aging and vision. *Vision Research*, 51(13), 1610–22. doi:10.1016/j.visres.2010.10.020

Petersen, S. E., & Posner, M. I. (2012). The attention system of the human brain: 20 years after. *Annual Review of Neuroscience*, 35, 73–89. doi:10.1146/annurev-neuro-062111-150525

Pletzer, B., Scheuringer, A., & Scherndl, T. (2017). Global-local processing relates to spatial and verbal processing: implications for sex differences in cognition. *Scientific Reports*, 7(1), 10575. doi:10.1038/s41598-017-11013-6

Pomerantz, J. R. (1983). Global and local precedence: selective attention in form and motion perception. *Journal of Experimental Psychology: General*, *112*(4), 516–40.

Pomerantz, J. R., & Schwaitzberg, S. D. (1975). Grouping by proximity: Selective attention measures. *Perception & Psychophysics*, *18*(5), 355–61. doi:10.3758/bf03211212

Posner, M. I. (1980). Orienting of attention. *The Quarterly Journal of Experimental Psychology*, *32*(1), 3–25. doi:10.1080/00335558008248231

Posner, M. I., & Cohen, Y. (1984). Components of visual orienting. In H. Bouma & D. Bouwhuis, eds., *Attention & Performance X*, Hillsdale: Erlbaum, pp. 531–56.

Posner, M. I., & Rothbart, M. K. (2007). Research on attention networks as a model for the integration of psychological science. *Annual Review of Psychology*, *58*, 1–23. doi:10.1146/annurev.psych.58.110405.085516

Posner, M. I., Snyder, C. R. R., & Davidson, B. J. (1980). Attention and the detection of signals. *Journal of Experimental Psychology: General*, *109*(2), 160–74. doi:10.1037/0096-3445.109.2.160

Pringle, H. L., Irwin, D. E., Kramer, A. F., & Atchley, P. (2001). The role of attentional breadth in perceptual change detection. *Psychonomic Bulletin & Review*, *8*(1), 89–95. doi:10.3758/bf03196143

Prinzmetal, W., McCool, C., & Park, S. (2005). Attention: reaction time and accuracy reveal different mechanisms. *Journal of Experimental Psychology: General*, *134*(1), 73–92. doi:10.1037/0096-3445.134.1.73

Prinzmetal, W., Zvinyatskovskiy, A., Gutierrez, P., & Dilem, L. (2009). Voluntary and involuntary attention have different consequences: the effect of perceptual difficulty. *Quarterly Journal of Experimental Psychology*, *62*(2), 352–69. doi:10.1080/17470210801954892

Proud, M., Goodhew, S. C., & Edwards, M. (2020). A vigilance avoidance account of spatial selectivity in dual-stream emotion induced blindness. *Psychonomic Bulletin & Review*. doi:10.3758/s13423-019-01690-x

Raymond, J. E., Shapiro, K. L., & Arnell, K. M. (1992). Temporary suppression of visual processing in an RSVP task: An attentional blink? *Journal of Experimental Psychology: Human Perception and Performance*, *18*(3), 849–60. doi:10.1037/0096-1523.18.3.849

Richard, A. M., Lee, H., & Vecera, S. P. (2008). Attentional spreading in object-based attention. *Journal of Experimental Psychology: General*, *34*(4), 842–53. doi:10.1037/0096-1523.34.4.842

Robertson, L. C. (1996). Attentional persistence for features of hierarchical patterns. *Journal of Experimental Psychology: General*, *125*(3), 227–49. doi:10.1037/0096-3445.125.3.227

Robertson, L. C., Egly, R., Lamb, M. R., & Kerth, L. (1993). Spatial attention and cuing to global and local levels of hierarchical structure. *Journal of Experimental Psychology: Human Perception and Performance, 19*(3), 471–87. doi:10.1037//0096-1523.19.3.471

Roenker, D. L., Cissell, G. M., Ball, K. K., Wadley, V. G., & Edwards, J. D. (2003). Speed-of-processing and driving simulator training result in improved driving performance. *Hum Factors, 45*(2), 218–33. doi:10.1518/hfes.45.2.218.27241

Rowe, G., Hirsh, J. B., & Anderson, A. K. (2007). Positive affect increases the breadth of attentional selection. *Proceedings of the National Academy of Sciences, 104*(1), 383–8. doi:10.1073/pnas.0605198104

Sasaki, Y., Hadjikhani, N., Fischl, B., Liu, A. K., Marret, S., Dale, A. M., & Tootell, R. B. H. (2001). Local and global attention are mapped retinotopically in human occipital cortex. *Proceedings of the National Academy of Sciences, 98*(4), 2077–82. doi:10.1073/pnas.98.4.2077

Schiller, P. H., & Logothetis, N. K. (1990). The color-opponent and broad-band channels of the primate visual system. *Trends in Neurosciences, 13*(10), 392–8. doi:10.1016/0166-2236(90)90117-s

Schiller, P. H., Logothetis, N. K., & Charles, E. R. (1990). Functions of the color-opponent and broad-band channels of the visual-system. *Nature, 343* (6253), 68–70. doi:10.1038/343068a0

Sekuler, R., & Ball, K. (1986). Visual localization: age and practice. *Journal of the Optical Society of America A, 3*(6), 864–7. doi:10.1364/JOSAA.3.000864

Senzaki, S., Masuda, T., & Nand, K. (2014). Holistic Versus Analytic Expressions in Artworks: Cross-Cultural Differences and Similarities in Drawings and Collages by Canadian and Japanese School-Age Children. *Journal of cross-cultural psychology, 45*(8), 1297–316. doi:10.1177/0022022114537704

Seya, Y., Nakayasu, H., & Yagi, T. (2013). Useful Field of View in Simulated Driving: Reaction Times and Eye Movements of Drivers. *i-Perception, 4*(4), 285–98. doi:10.1068/i0512

Shomstein, S., Lee, J., & Behrmann, M. (2010). Top-down and bottom-up attentional guidance: investigating the role of the dorsal and ventral parietal cortices. *Experimental Brain Research, 206*(2), 197–208. doi:10.1007/s00221-010-2326-z

Shulman, G. L., Sullivan, M. A., Gish, K., & Sakoda, W. J. (1986). The role of spatial-frequency channels in the perception of local and global structure. *Perception, 15*(3), 259–73. doi:10.1068/p150259

Spearman, C. (1910). CORRELATION CALCULATED FROM FAULTY DATA. *British Journal of Psychology, 1904–1920, 3*(3), 271–295. doi: doi:10.1111/j.2044-8295.1910.tb00206.x

Srinivasan, N., & Hanif, A. (2010). Global-happy and local-sad: Perceptual processing affects emotion identification. *Cognition and Emotion, 24*(6), 1062–9. doi:10.1080/02699930903101103

Stoffer, T. H. (1993). The time course of attentional zooming: a comparison of voluntary and involuntary allocation of attention to the levels of compound stimuli. *Psychological Research, 56*(1), 14–25.

Tanaka, K., & Saito, H. (1989). Analysis of motion of the visual field by direction, expansion/ contraction, and rotation cells clustered in the dorsal part of the medial superior temporal area of the macaque monkey. *J Neurophysiol, 62*(3), 626–41. doi:10.1152/jn.1989.62.3.626

Taylor, C. T., Cross, K., & Amir, N. (2016). Attentional control moderates the relationship between social anxiety symptoms and attentional disengagement from threatening information. *Journal of Behavior Therapy and Experimental Psychiatry, 50,* 68–76. doi:10.1016/j.jbtep.2015.05.008

Taylor, J. E., Chan, D., Bennett, P. J., & Pratt, J. (2015). Attentional cartography: mapping the distribution of attention across time and space. *Attention Perception & Psychophysics, 77*(7), 2240–6. doi:10.3758/s13414-015-0943-0

Thomas, L. E. (2015). Grasp Posture Alters Visual Processing Biases Near the Hands. *Psychological Science, 26*(5), 625–32. doi:10.1177/0956797615571418

Vogel, E. K., & Luck, S. J. (2000). The visual N1 component as an index of a discrimination process. *Psychophysiology, 37*(2), 190–203. doi:10.1111/1469-8986.3720190

Ward, L. M. (1982). Determinants of attention to local and global features of visual forms. *Journal of Experimental Psychology: Human Perception and Performance, 8*(4), 562–81. doi:10.1037/0096-1523.8.4.562

White, C. N., Ratcliff, R., & Starns, J. S. (2011). Diffusion models of the flanker task: Discrete versus gradual attentional selection. *Cognitive Psychology, 63*(4), 210–38. doi:10.1016/j.cogpsych.2011.08.001

Wilkinson, D. T., Halligan, P. W., Marshall, J. C., Büchel, C., & Dolan, R. J. (2001). Switching between the Forest and the Trees: Brain Systems Involved in Local/Global Changed-Level Judgments. *NeuroImage, 13*(1), 56–67. doi: doi.org/10.1006/nimg.2000.0678

Wilson, K. E., Lowe, M. X., Ruppel, J., Pratt, J., & Ferber, S. (2016). The scope of no return: Openness predicts the spatial distribution of Inhibition of

Return. *Attention, Perception & Psychophysics, 78*, 209–17. doi:10.3758/s13414-015-0991-5

Wood, J. M., Chaparro, A., Lacherez, P., & Hickson, L. (2012). Useful field of view predicts driving in the presence of distracters. *Optom Vis Sci, 89*(4), 373–81. doi:10.1097/OPX.0b013e31824c17ee

Yeshurun, Y., & Carrasco, M. (1998). Attention improves or impairs visual performance by enhancing spatial resolution. *Nature, 396*(6706), 72–5. doi:10.1038/23936

Yeshurun, Y., & Carrasco, M. (2008). The effects of transient attention on spatial resolution and the size of the attentional cue. *Perception & Psychophysics, 70*(1), 104–13. doi:10.3758/PP.70.1.104

Yeshurun, Y., & Levy, L. (2003). Transient spatial attention degrades temporal resolution. *Psychological Science, 14*(3), 225–31. doi:10.1111/1467-9280.02436

Yeshurun, Y., & Marom, G. (2008). Transient spatial attention and the perceived duration of brief visual events. *Visual Cognition, 16*(6), 826–48. doi:10.1080/13506280701588022

Yeshurun, Y., Montagna, B., & Carrasco, M. (2008). On the flexibility of sustained attention and its effects on a texture segmentation task. *Vision Research, 48*(1), 80–95. doi:10.1016/j.visres.2007.10.015

Yeshurun, Y., & Sabo, G. (2012). Differential effects of transient attention on inferred parvocellular and magnocellular processing. *Vision Research, 74*, 21–9. doi:10.1016/j.visres.2012.06.006

Yovel, G., Levy, J., & Yovel, I. (2001). Hemispheric asymmetries for global and local visual perception: effects of stimulus and task factors. *Journal of Experimental Psychology: Human Perception and Performance, 27*(6), 1369–85. doi:10.1037/0096-1523.27.6.1369

Zvielli, A., Bernstein, A., & Koster, E. H. W. (2015). Temporal Dynamics of Attentional Bias. *Clinical Psychological Science, 3*(5), 772–88. doi:10.1177/2167702614551572

Acknowledgements

This work was supported by an Australian Research Council Future Fellowship (FT170100021) awarded to SCG. I thank Mark Edwards for helpful comments during the development of this Element. I also thank members of the Visual Cognition Lab for insightful discussions.

Cambridge Elements ≡

Perception

James T. Enns
The University of British Columbia

Editor James T. Enns is Professor at the University of British Columbia, where he researches the interaction of perception, attention, emotion, and social factors. He has previously been Editor of the *Journal of Experimental Psychology: Human Perception and Performance* and an Associate Editor at *Psychological Science, Consciousness and Cognition, Attention Perception & Psychophysics*, and *Visual Cognition*.

About the Series

The modern study of human perception includes event perception, bidirectional influences between perception and action, music, language, the integration of the senses, human action observation, and the important roles of emotion, motivation, and social factors. Each Element in the series combines authoritative literature reviews of foundational topics with forward-looking presentations of the recent developments on a given topic.

Perception

Printed in the United States
By Bookmasters